Routledge Revivals

David Mamet

First published in 1985, C.W.E Bigsby examines the career and work of playwright David Mamet. Bigsby shows that Mamet is a fierce social critic, indicting an America corrupted at its core by myths of frontier individualism and competitive capitalism. Mamet has created plays whose bleak social vision and ironic metaphysics are redeemed, if at all, by the power of imagination. No American playwright before him has displayed the same sensitivity to language, detecting lyricism in the brutal incoherencies of every day speech and investing with meaning a contemporary aphasia. Few have offered dramatic metaphors of such startling and disturbing originality. Bigsby's study is the first book to provide a thorough account of David Mamet's life and career, as well as close analyses of individual plays.

David Mamet

C.W.E. Bigsby

First published in 1985
by Methuen

This edition first published in 2018 by Routledge
2 Park Square, Milton Park, Abingdon, Oxon, OX14 4RN
and by Routledge
711 Third Avenue, New York, NY 10017

Routledge is an imprint of the Taylor & Francis Group, an informa business

© 1985 David Mamet

All rights reserved. No part of this book may be reprinted or reproduced or utilised in any form or by any electronic, mechanical, or other means, now known or hereafter invented, including photocopying and recording, or in any information storage or retrieval system, without permission in writing from the publishers.

Publisher's Note
The publisher has gone to great lengths to ensure the quality of this reprint but points out that some imperfections in the original copies may be apparent.

Disclaimer
The publisher has made every effort to trace copyright holders and welcomes correspondence from those they have been unable to contact.
A Library of Congress record exists under the ISBN: 85015234

ISBN 13: 978-1-138-55694-2 (hbk)
ISBN 13: 978-1-315-15065-9 (ebk)
ISBN 13: 978-1-138-55712-3 (pbk)

CONTEMPORARY WRITERS

General Editors
MALCOLM BRADBURY
and
CHRISTOPHER BIGSBY

DAVID MAMET

IN THE SAME SERIES

Donald Barthelme *M. Couturier and R. Durand*
Saul Bellow *Malcolm Bradbury*
Richard Brautigan *Marc Chénetier*
E. L. Doctorow *Paul Levine*
Margaret Drabble *Joanne V. Creighton*
John Fowles *Peter Conradi*
Günter Grass *Ronald Hayman*
Graham Greene *John Spurling*
Seamus Heaney *Blake Morrison*
Ted Hughes *Thomas West*
Philip Larkin *Andrew Motion*
Doris Lessing *Lorna Sage*
Malcolm Lowry *Ronald Binns*
Iris Murdoch *Richard Todd*
Joe Orton *C. W. E. Bigsby*
Harold Pinter *G. Almansi and S. Henderson*
Thomas Pynchon *Tony Tanner*
Alain Robbe-Grillet *John Fletcher*
Philip Roth *Hermione Lee*
Kurt Vonnegut *Jerome Klinkowitz*
Patrick White *John Colmer*

DAVID MAMET

C. W. E. BIGSBY

METHUEN
LONDON AND NEW YORK

First published in 1985 by
Methuen & Co. Ltd
11 New Fetter Lane, London EC4P 4EE
Published in the USA by
Methuen & Co.
in association with Methuen, Inc.
29 West 35th Street, New York, NY 1001

© 1985 C. W. E. Bigsby

Typeset by Rowland Phototypesetting Ltd

All rights reserved. No part of this book may be reprinted or reproduced or utilized in any form or by any electronic, mechanical or other means, now known or hereafter invented, including photocopying and recording, or in any information storage or retrieval system, without permission in writing from the publishers.

British Library Cataloguing in Publication Data

Bigsby, C. W. E.
David Mamet. – (Contemporary writers)
1. Mamet, David – Criticism and interpretation
I. Title II. Series
812'.54 PS3563.A434/

ISBN 0-416-40980-6

Library of Congress Cataloging in Publication Data

Bigsby, C. W. E.
David Mamet.
(Contemporary writers)
Bibliography: p.
1. Mamet, David – Criticism and interpretation
I. Title II. Series
PS3563.A4345Z55   1985   812'.54   85-15234

ISBN 0-416-40980-6 (pbk.)

CONTENTS

General editors' preface 6
Acknowledgements 8
A note on the texts 9

1 Beginnings 11
2 Story and anti-story: *Lakeboat, Duck Variations, Dark Pony, Reunion, The Disappearance of the Jews* 22
3 *Sexual Perversity in Chicago, The Woods* 46
4 *American Buffalo* 63
5 *The Water Engine, A Life in the Theatre* 86
6 The culture of narcissism: *Edmond* 101
7 *Glengarry, Glen Ross* 111
8 Conclusions 127

Notes 137
Bibliography 141

GENERAL EDITORS' PREFACE

The contemporary is a country which we all inhabit, but there is little agreement as to its boundaries or its shape. The serious writer is one of its most sensitive interpreters, but criticism is notoriously cautious in offering a response or making a judgement. Accordingly, this continuing series is an endeavour to look at some of the most important writers of our time, and the questions raised by their work. It is, in effect, an attempt to map the contemporary, to describe its aesthetic and moral topography.

The series came into existence out of two convictions. One was that, despite all the modern pressures on the writer and on literary culture, we live in a major creative time, as vigorous and alive in its distinctive way as any that went before. The other was that, though criticism itself tends to grow more theoretical and apparently indifferent to contemporary creation, there are grounds for a lively aesthetic debate. This series, which includes books written from various standpoints, is meant to provide a forum for that debate. By design, some of those who have contributed are themselves writers, willing to respond to their contemporaries; others are critics who have brought to the discussion of current writing the spirit of contemporary criticism or simply a conviction, forcibly and coherently argued, for the contemporary significance of their subjects. Our aim, as the series develops, is to continue to explore the works of major post-war writers – in fiction, drama and poetry – over an international range, and thereby to illuminate not only those works but also in some degree the artistic, social and moral assumptions on which they rest. Our wish is that, in their very variety of approach and emphasis, these books will stimulate interest in and understanding of the vitality of a living literature which, because it is contemporary, is especially ours.

Norwich, England　　　　　　　　　　　MALCOLM BRADBURY
　　　　　　　　　　　　　　　　　　　　CHRISTOPHER BIGSBY

ACKNOWLEDGEMENTS

I wish to acknowledge David Mamet's kindness in submitting to two interviews, one in London and one in Vermont, and for making available to me unpublished plays and essays.

A NOTE ON THE TEXTS

Page references to Mamet's plays are from the American editions of his plays, with the exception of *Duck Variations*, *Sexual Perversity in Chicago* and *American Buffalo*, where the Methuen edition was used.

1

BEGINNINGS

By the early 1970s the American theatre seemed in one of its periodic crises. The promise of Off- and Off-Off-Broadway had largely dissipated; its leading companies had closed, and the social and political pressures which had given it a special significance for the best part of a decade had relaxed. It was no longer possible to pretend that the theatre was at the heart of a debate about central moral issues or was conducting a radical revision of artistic form. Meanwhile, the major figures of the American theatre, Arthur Miller, Tennessee Williams and Edward Albee – people who had between them dominated the 1940s, 1950s and 1960s – seemed to disappear from public view. Miller's *The Price* was reasonably well received in 1968, but appeared at the time to be a coda to his career. Williams, in deep personal crisis throughout much of the sixties, produced a string of disappointing, even shrill works. Albee increasingly opted for arcane experiments which detached him from his audience. With rapidly increasing costs, Broadway was less willing than ever to present the work of new American playwrights, preferring musicals, comedies and British imports already tested out in London's West End. As one young writer lamented:

> The critical establishment doesn't like it unless it's foreign. Tolstoy once said about the Russian army – when a general had achieved the highest rank he could as a Russian, they promoted him to a German. It's almost like that in this country. The highest you could achieve was to be thought an honorary Englishman, because we don't feel that our actual life is a fit subject for drama.[1]

That writer, born in what he himself called the 'city state of Chicago' and living in Vermont – 'a country between the United States and Canada' – was David Mamet, whose work has addressed not only the 'actual life' of Americans but also the fantasies with which they choose to cloak that life and the language with which they express what he sees as its growing anxiety and desperation. Behind the whimsy of these comments, there is a more serious point: Mamet here seems to claim an ironic detachment from the business and the busyness of America which is not unrelated to the tone and stance of his drama. Despite the fact that he has since had his work successfully produced on Broadway – achievement in regional theatre becoming, in the 1970s and 1980s, a primary route on to the Great White Way – he remains in many respects at odds with its values, as he does with those of a society which he regards as 'very, very nuts'. Beyond his central concern with the craft of theatre and its power to shape experience, language and thought, his plays stand as a consistent critique of a country whose public myths he regards as destructive, and whose deep lack of communality he finds disturbing.

Though his first plays – *Duck Variations* (1972) and *Sexual Perversity in Chicago* (1973) – were well received in Chicago, neither they nor the subsequent *American Buffalo* (1975) earned him immediate national attention. But when, in 1977, the last-mentioned play did open on Broadway, it was in a year that four of his plays received their première in theatres across America: *Dark Pony* at Yale Rep, *The Water Engine* and *The Woods* in Chicago, and *A Life in the Theatre* in New York. Profoundly different from one another, they posed genuine problems for critics trying to make sense of a writer whose theatrical effectiveness was undeniable, but whose precise achievement left them baffled. When he followed these with *Lakeboat* (1979), a work originally written in 1970, the chronological confusion did little to help. In fact, critics and reviewers have always found David Mamet difficult to pin down. At first they were often shocked by the language of his characters, and bemused by a mixture of styles which seemed to range from impressionism to naturalism. The plays themselves varied from absurdist parables to bitter social critiques. There was often a grudging admiration for the precision of his social observation but some confusion about the real strength of his work and the direction of his career. Even *American Buffalo* was none too well received at the time of its New York début, though, by the time it was revived six years later, it was widely regarded as a classic of the American theatre. By some legerdemain Mamet had become a mainstay of the American theatre almost by stealth. However, though he now commands high critical respect, and in 1984 won the Pulitzer Prize with *Glengarry, Glen Ross*, there remains a sense in which he continues to bemuse those who resist his concern for metaphor and his fascination with character as a product of language and social myth.

Thus Henry Hewes objected of *American Buffalo*, which he otherwise admired, that 'I don't think that really an awful lot has happened',[2] while John Simon insisted that 'I'm not asking for unity of action, I'm asking for any bloody kind of action whatsoever.'[3] Walter Kerr regretted that Mamet was seemingly drawn to the language of the semi-literate and characterized *Duck Variations* and *Reunion* as merely conversation pieces, *A Life in the Theatre* as an atmospheric study, *Sexual Perversity in Chicago* as an impressionistic montage and *American Buffalo* as a genre-cum-language exercise. Indeed, he began to wonder whether he had 'any gift for forward movement, for sustained drama, for, in short, story-telling.' Of *The Water Engine*, which he admired, Richard Eder confessed that 'Just what the truffle is I don't know', as Kerr had expressed bafflement over his choice of structure. In fact, few playwrights have paid more attention to language, to the force of dramatic metaphor, to structure or to character as expression of psychological or social dislocation. None has given storytelling quite such a central role as method and subject. Since he writes about those who are representatives of a social class 'who create nothing [and] do nothing', it is scarcely surprising that he should have explored a hermeticism which Henry Hewes resisted, disturbed by what he took to be the 'circular shape' of his plays. This is not to say that there is no development within those plays, merely that to look for it in an unravelling plot or the exposure of hidden truths is to look in the wrong place. Mamet's dramatic metaphors work by accretion, a slow intensifying of meaning. Action is character; action is also a language whose rhythms, tonalities, intensities and silences generate and reveal crucial anxieties. Mamet, too, believes in the necessity to 'forward the action' and recognizes the compulsion to discover 'what happens next'; it is simply that a play's energy may subsist in more than the unwinding of narrative logic. Eugene Ionesco once observed that all plays are in essence detective stories, and there are to be sure mysteries to be solved here, too; but their exposure has rather less to do with action as a sequence of events than as a product of the words we speak, or forbear to speak, the fictions we elaborate, the shifting relationships which suggest a change in the balance of psychological or social power. He is, he has insisted, not interested in simply serving the interests of the plot: 'if it's not poetic on the stage, forget it.'[4] For him, 'Rhythm and action are the same'; 'in the theatre, if you have to use any narration, you're not doing your job.'[5]

What kind of playwright is Mamet? The pedigree of his first public success, *Duck Variations*, seemed obvious enough, owing something to Edward Albee and something to Samuel Beckett. But *Sexual Perversity in Chicago* was different; to many its language seemed obscene, its structure fragmented, its rhythms unfamiliar and its characters socially marginal and morally suspect. *American Buffalo* proved even more of a shock, its violence of expression and, occasionally, action being too readily accommodated to a naturalistic tradition. Initially, at least, it was seen as little more than a glimpse of the underworld, faithfully transcribing its argot and accurately reproducing its determinisms. What was, for the most part, missed was the degree to which Mamet, in this play, presents the social world less as fact than as image, sees in the etiolated language of his characters evidence simultaneously of a damaged social self and a fragmented moral experience, and generates a lyrical counterpoint out of the very incompletions which are the product of alienation. Though it was praised or attacked as a modern-day version of *The Lower Depths*, its subject was, in some fundamental sense, history and the way people have betrayed it and it has betrayed them. The sense of theatrical stasis which so distressed some critics (not much happens in terms of stage action until a sudden spasm of violence at the end) was a natural corollary of a moral and spiritual paralysis which has very little to do with the determinisms implicit in the naturalistic vision. The scatological vocabulary was an entirely familiar fact of urban living, albeit one which, even in the 1970s, seldom found its way into the theatre, but there was something about a sexually charged language drained of its sexual content which raised it from realistic detail to prophetic symbol as it expressed his sense of an impotent, potentially terminal, culture. None the less it was not for that he was praised. He was welcomed and disparaged as a simple realist whose accomplishment lay in capturing and reproducing a particular kind of urban aphasia. His real achievement lay elsewhere.

Thoreau observed that 'The cost of a thing is the amount of what I will call life which is to be exchanged for it, immediately or in the long run.'[6] This has essentially been Mamet's central theme throughout a career in which his theatrical inventiveness, his linguistic subtlety, his ability to forge powerful images of alienation and create lyrical tone poems of striking effect, have established him as a major force in contemporary drama. That it took some time for his significance to be acknowledged is perhaps scarcely surprising in a theatre which too often has had to settle for the ersatz, and a culture whose pieties he has set himself to assault.

Mamet's critics have largely seen him as seizing on the externals of American life – speech patterns, social class, physical detail – but his actual concern has been with dramatizing the inner life of the individual and the nation. He is, to be sure, interested in what Hawthorne called 'The Present, the Immediate, the Actual' but only in so far as these can be reshaped into metaphor. He is a moralist lamenting the collapse of public form and private purpose, exposing a spiritually desiccated world in which the cadences of despair predominate, and the occasional consonance offered by relationship or the momentary lyricism buried deep inside the structure of language implies little more than an echo of what was once a state of grace. But that grace does lie far back in the past, beyond a century and more of violence and betrayal. His target is, in effect, less American realities than the myths that have deformed American possibility. Since the possession of the American continent can be seen both as an enabling myth and as an act of theft validated by rhetoric detached from its moral roots, the inheritors of that history find themselves the dubious beneficiaries of an ambiguous birthright. The supposed frontier virtues of a sturdy masculine self-sufficiency that took by force what was denied by right are echoed in his plays by people who deploy that rhetoric and dispose those myths in a world that has lost its epic dimensions. Perhaps the myths were always crude rationalizations, but at least the sheer scale on which they were enacted sustained the elevated language and concealed the extent of the moral affront. But, mimicked in his plays by the petty gangster and the salesman, they become ironic as well as immoral, while their deforming effect on the individual and the culture becomes more clearly apparent in the pettiness of their projects and the patently self-destructive nature of their fantasies.

In fact, there is a powerful sense of betrayal in his drama – the sense of a promise not merely unfulfilled but denied by the very attempt to seize it presumptuously. Just how he manages to combine jeremiad with celebration is one of the mysteries of David Mamet. For if he pins America dispassionately to its corruptions and treasons, if he chooses to dramatize the results of a wilful surrender of national purpose and personal meaning, he also forges poetry out of the sludge of language left behind by a century and more of public lies and private collusion. Creating characters who bear the weight of self-justifying fantasies, Mamet is also fascinated by their capacity for invention, their irrepressible effort to bend the world into the shape demanded by an imagination that seems to have outlived both will and moral sense. Old and New Testaments coexist, with threats of an impending apocalypse held at bay by a redemptive compassion.

Admonition and admiration are, after all, not the strange bedfellows they may seem. Walt Whitman was one writer who managed to maintain that tension, and there is a touch of Whitman in Mamet – in his inclusiveness, his wit, the tendency of his prose to align itself into verse, and the almost religious tone of his denunciation of material and spiritual corruption. The author of *American Buffalo* and *Glengarry, Glen Ross* would certainly have little difficulty in recognizing his kinship with the man who wrote:

> The depravity of the business classes in our country is not less than has been supposed, but infinitely greater. . . . The great cities rich with respectable as much as non-respectable robbery and scoundrelism. In fashionable life, flippancy, tepid amours, weak infidelism, small aims, or no aims at all, only to kill time, in business (this all-devouring modern word, business), the one sole object is, by any means, pecuniary gain. . . . Money-making . . . [remains] today sole master of the field. . . . In vain do we march with unprecedented strides to empire. . . . It is as if we were somehow being endowed with a vast and more thoroughly-appointed body, and then left with little or no soul.[7]

The irony of Mamet's characters derives not from a collapse of faith in the American dream but from the persistence of that faith beyond reason, and from the prosaic nature of the dream they choose to embrace. All the evidence suggests a culture that has traded in its vision for the trinkets of modern civilization (for hard cash in *American Buffalo*, for a Cadillac and a set of steak knives in *Glengarry, Glen Ross*) or immediate sexual gratification (in *Sexual Perversity in Chicago* and *Edmond*); however, virtually all of his characters continue to sense the need for something more, for some meaning which their language cannot encompass, but which they struggle to articulate in a hand-me-down vocabulary that hints at humane values and a liberal faith lost somewhere back in an American past plundered for its rhetoric but denied as the source of values. It was the Chicago writer Henry Blake Fuller who had a character say of Chicago, the setting for many of Mamet's plays, that it

> labors under one great disadvantage: it is the only great city in the world in which all its citizens have come for the one common, avowed object of making money. There you have its genesis, its growth, its end, its object. . . . In this Garden City of ours every man cultivates his own little bed and his neighbor his; but who looks after the paths between?[8]

David Mamet's concern is precisely with these paths between.

*

Mamet is an urban writer. The city (usually Chicago, sometimes New York) provides his subject, and generates the rhythm of his plays and the demotic energy of his characters. He writes, for the most part, about the spiritually dispossessed, about people who are the alienated products of capitalism ('an idea whose time has come and gone'), and of their substitution of fantasy for will, sensation for relationship. He sets out to dramatize a society that seems to have severed its links with the past (which survives only as debased myth) and to lack a vision of the future (except in its vague promises of sexual, moral and material liberation). His are characters who live their lives through a series of denials, and in that sense, at least, his own family background seems paradigmatic:

> My grandparents were Russian-Jewish immigrants. My father grew up poor but subsequently made a good living. My life was expunged of any tradition at all. Nothing old in the house. No colour in the house. The virtues expounded were not creative but remedial; let's stop being Jewish, let's stop being poor.

A 1982 play was actually called *The Disappearance of the Jews*. His response to this background to the tedium of his school life was to create an alternative world: 'Anything that wasn't official, I knew that's where I wanted to be. . . . I had to invent my own life and my own fun.'[9] That process did not merely lead him to theatre; it also gave him a central dramatic theme. In play after play he creates characters in some way detached from history, people who are themselves compulsive fictionalizers, desperately reshaping their experiences in such a way as to deny the reality of their own anxieties and the anxiety inspired by reality.

David Mamet was born in Chicago in 1947, and brought up in the Jewish area of the South Side. His mother (who early accused him of 'dramatizing things . . . making up stories') was a teacher, his father a labour lawyer and amateur semanticist (Mamet learned children's rhymes from a recording produced by the International Society for Semantics). When his parents were divorced, Mamet lived with his mother and attended a private school in the Chicago suburb of Olympia Fields. While he was studying at this school, he worked for a time at the Hull

House Theatre (an amateur group directed by Bob Sickinger) and, as a general kitchen help, at Chicago's improvisational theatre, Second City, a group which fostered such talents as Mike Nichols, Elaine May and Alan Arkin and which Mamet later regarded as having a crucial influence on his own work and as having invented a new kind of theatre – fast-paced, improvisational, episodic, satirical. But his childhood connection with theatre was rather more direct. His uncle was the Director of Broadcasting for the Chicago Board of Rabbis; for a time Mamet appeared on television, playing Jewish children with religious problems. When he went to university – Goddard College in Plainfield, Vermont – it seemed natural to choose to major in literature and theatre; and it was here that he wrote his first play – a revue called *Camel* – to fulfil his thesis requirement in English literature. It was then too that he took an eighteen-month break (1968–9) to study at the Neighborhood Playhouse, a Stanislavsky-oriented company under Sanford Meisner, a founder member of the Group Theatre of the 1930s. This experience, he later insisted, taught him the degree to which 'the language we use, its rhythm, actually determines the way we behave rather than the other way around'.[10] His ambitions as an actor, however, quickly foundered, failing to survive a period spent working New England's summer stock theatre.

Throughout this period the Vietnam war was at its height. Mamet himself was never drafted, first because of a college deferment, then because of a mental breakdown (an experience about which he consistently refuses to speak but which seems to surface in his work in a concern for those in a state bordering on psychosis). He played little or no role in the anti-war movement, a fact that is perhaps the source of a residual guilt; he has certainly expressed the hope and conviction that, placed in a similar situation again, he would be more active. It is tempting to see the acerbity of his social criticism, his desire to be seen as a social playwright, as partly a response to what he plainly feels to have been his failure to address the principal moral issue of his generation. Certainly one literary tradition to which he wishes to lay claim is that constituted by such Chicago or Midwestern writers as Frank Norris, Theodore Dreiser, Willa Cather (his daughter is called Willa), Sinclair

Lewis and Upton Sinclair. He admires them in part for their commitment to capturing the rhythms of the new urban environment but, more importantly, for what he sees as their prophetic nature. Writing at a time when America was inclined to celebrate its material achievements and to see the machine age as ushering in a new century of material prosperity and spiritual fulfilment, they saw beyond the immediate and probed beneath the surface of American confidence, challenging, as Mamet does too, dominant assumptions about the nature of the real and the desirable.

At the same time, his fascination with language, with character seen outside the context of event, with the self-sustaining fictions and performances of those for whom story and survival are intimately related, owes rather more to European origins. It is true that O'Neill, Miller, Williams and Albee have all created characters who are themselves compulsive fictionalizers – and they, too, are a felt presence behind the characters in *American Buffalo*, *A Life in the Theatre* and several of his other plays – but his exploration of stasis, his belief in the critical importance of absence and his desire to redefine the use of language, character and plot, relate his work more directly to Beckett and Pinter, whose work he greatly admires. More than most American writers, he bridges both traditions, combining social satire with metaphysics, a scatological language with lyricism, the disjunctive rhythms of urban life with a meticulous concern for form.

Mamet completed his degree in 1969, and for a short time worked as an actor. He was also stage manager for the long-running Off-Broadway musical, *The Fantasticks*. But, like so many other American writers, his credentials also include rather more mundane work: in his time he has been employed in a truck factory, a canning plant and a real-estate agency (the last providing the material for *Glengarry, Glen Ross*), and has been an office cleaner, a window washer and a taxi driver. Apart from anything else, these experiences have given him a sensitivity to the American vernacular unequalled by any other playwright, but they also alerted him to what he sees as the profound alienation which typifies an urban America in which activity is detached from meaning and desires are unrelated to human need.

After a short hiatus he worked briefly as drama teacher at Marlboro College, Vermont. Then, after a succession of other jobs, he returned to Goddard College, where he worked as an instructor and began writing plays for use in his acting classes. Partly as a result of this he founded a small drama group, the St Nicholas Company, which performed both his work and that of others. In 1972 he returned to Chicago.

His early work was produced by a number of small Chicago-based groups: *Duck Variations* by the Body Politic; a children's play called *Mackinac* and a play set in Lisbon at the time of the Inquisition, *Marranos*, by a Jewish community centre. Then came *Sexual Perversity in Chicago*. The play's success (it was voted best new Chicago play) finally convinced him that he was a dramatist, rather than an actor who simply wrote on the side. But that success was still only a Chicago affair. When he sent copies of his plays to Joe Papp in New York he got no response ('Coming from Chicago, it was as if the scripts didn't travel well. . . . They were funny and sad in Chicago, but the vibrations of the train disturbed them on their way to New York'[11]). In 1974 he re-established the St Nicholas Company, now renamed the St Nicholas Players (he resigned from it two years later because of disagreements with his co-founders). They performed two more of his plays – *Squirrels*, which was concerned with the problems of a writer, and a comic children's play called *The Poet and the Rent*. Then, in 1975, he finally succeeded in having his work staged in New York. *Duck Variations* and *Sexual Perversity in Chicago* opened at the St Clements Theatre, the latter winning an Obie Award as the best play of the year. The production moved to the Cherry Lane Theatre and paved the way for the Broadway run, in 1977, of *American Buffalo* – voted best play of the year by the New York Drama Critics. Despite the new importance of regional theatre, it was still success in New York which established a national reputation; contemptuous as he was of such a system and, indeed, as *Edmond* (1982) was to show, of New York itself, it was success in New York that he sought.

2

STORY AND ANTI-STORY: 'LAKEBOAT', 'DUCK VARIATIONS', 'DARK PONY', 'REUNION', 'THE DISAPPEARANCE OF THE JEWS'

In an essay on Chekhov, Thomas Mann remarked that 'All his work was honorable sleeplessness, a search for the right, redeeming word in answer to the question: "What are we to do?" The word was difficult, if not impossible, to find.' What he substituted, according to Mann, was the conviction that 'One "entertains a forlorn world by telling stories without ever being able to offer it the trace of a saving truth."'[12] For David Mamet, an admirer of Chekhov's work, storytelling also becomes fundamental, not only a central strategy of the writer, struggling to give coherence to a chaotic experience, but also a basic tactic of characters for whom it becomes a resource, a retreat and ultimately the only available redemption, if only because it implies the minimal community of taleteller and listener. (In a play, *Prairie du chien*, which he wrote for National Public Radio in 1979, the two principal characters are, indeed, a Story Teller and a Listener.) Because storytelling may be an act of evasion, it is at times ironic; because it may be an act of resistance, it is potentially the root of a limited transcendence. Mamet's world is peopled by individuals who are for the most part baffled and disturbed, aware of a need which they can hardly articulate or satisfy. The primary fact of their lives is a missing intimacy, and loss is his central theme. But in the face of this they compulsively elaborate fantasies, create plots, devise scenarios or simply exchange rumour and speculation. Story becomes a substitute for what is so manifestly absent from their own lives – a sense of coherence, meaning and communication. It also fills a silence which otherwise carries its own threat.

If this concern runs throughout his work, it was certainly there at the beginning in the play which he had mischievously listed on his curriculum vitae when he applied to Marlboro College, a play as yet unwritten – *Lakeboat*. First performed at the Theatre Workshop of Marlboro College in Vermont in 1970, it was later revised, with the co-operation of the artistic director of the Milwaukee Repertory Theater, and produced in 1979.

Lakeboat bears the marks of his experience with Second City in its episodic structure (there are twenty-eight scenes). It is set on a merchant marine ship, called the *T Harrison*, which sails on the Great Lakes. Although it is ostensibly a naturalistic study of life aboard ship, in the manner of the young Eugene O'Neill (whose plays Mamet had produced), this play, like the best of his work, erodes that naturalism, becoming in this case less a study of character and environment than an absurdist image, a dramatization of the attempt to give meaning and purpose to lives which lack both. In a sense *Lakeboat* is based on a cliché: life as a voyage. The boat is consciously offered as a microcosm. It is, as one of the characters remarks, 'The floating home of 45 men . . . a small world' (p. 24). Like the figures in Tom Stoppard's *Rosencrantz and Guildenstern are Dead*, those on board are condemned to a journey whose route is pre-ordained. In their case they travel between the various ports on the Great Lakes. Their only freedom is to choose how they will pass the time, or debate – like Rosencrantz and Guildenstern, no less than Beckett's Vladimir and Estragon – whether death might not be preferable. Absurdity attaches itself to both solutions. The only resource they can deploy lies in their fiction-making skills (in fact, largely nonexistent, since they adapt events to the models they have absorbed from the movies), a degree of protective wit and the fact of their shared fate.

Lakeboat consists of a series of conversations between those whose lives add up to little more than habitual actions interrupted by brief spasms of sex and drinking. The emptiness of their existence – one man watches a set of gauges for four hours at a stretch, another makes sandwiches, on a ship whose circular voyages mock the idea of a link between action and progress – is filled with memories and fantasies which merge, much as they do in Beckett's work. Virtually every encounter in *Lakeboat* involves storytelling, the play beginning with the Pierman asking: 'Did you hear about Skippy and the new kid?' (p. 17). That phrase, as a prelude to sometimes simple, sometimes elaborate, fictions, echoes throughout the piece:

> I heard it. I don't actually know it . . . Collins tells me . . . I heard the Cook has two Cadillacs . . . I heard that . . . I read it . . . I heard they might have drugged him . . . that's probably what happened . . . What'd you hear? . . . The way I hear it . . . It's just that I heard it . . .

Without a plot to their lives they fall back on invention. Simple statement quickly blooms into a narrative, an overheard remark into a drama. At the beginning of the play, we hear of the supposed mugging of the ship's night cook; by the end this has been elevated into an elaborate story of vice and crime. The absent cook becomes by turns a gambling degenerate left for dead by the Mafia and/or a powerful armed man killed by the FBI. The truth seems to be that he had simply overslept and missed the boat, though even this is a guess that carries conviction merely because it is closer to the banality of their existence. In other words, fiction is a fundamental strategy and consolation to characters who could scarcely survive the knowledge of their own marginality.

Mamet constructs the play from fragments of conversation, brief moments of apparent intimacy, accounts of blunted aspirations, the lies, delusions and self-deceits of characters drained of all transcendence. They debate the comparative virtues of film stars, investing their film roles with more substance and feeling than they grant to their own lives. They recall, with apparent pride, moments of drunkenness or crude sex; yet, beneath the brutalities, beyond the platitudes they exchange, are insecurities, fears and a sense of loss only hinted at in the monologues which pass for conversation and the hesitant gestures at friendship which they make. Thus Joe, still only an able-bodied seaman after a lifetime on the lakes, affects a pose of cynical worldliness, but toys with the idea of suicide, asking how long a man could survive in the icy waters of the lake and whether the ship carries morphine. And this is a clue to Mamet's method in the play. Like Chekhov, he seems to create a world in which time and causality are suspended. Characters talk, apparently idly, but behind the reassuring chatter there is a quiet desperation.

Mamet builds his picture by indirection. A remark is dropped here or there: in the middle of elaborate and generally secondhand stories of sexual conquest or dissipation the characters offer brief fragments of information about their lives, throwaway lines bearing little relation to the conversations they are having. Two men casually refer to the fact of their divorces, a third remarks on his mother's blindness. But the pain must be concealed, and the elaborate stories and mock-heroic accounts of sexual conquest are resumed, for such status as they have derives from the experience to which they can lay claim. Thus the fireman talks knowledgeably of guns, justifying his expertise by reference to his army service, a claim undercut by the nature of his assignment: 'I was in the Army. Overseas. Hawaii' (p. 92). Recognizing his mistaken precision, he adds, bathetically, 'But it wasn't a state.' The rhythm of his story, however, is such that it can sustain not merely unintentional irony but even flat contradiction:

FIREMAN. That boy drank. Used to drink on the ship.
FRED. Who doesn't?
FIREMAN. Not him, not him, for sure. (p. 93)

Statements are no sooner made than qualified or reversed ('He had it. I think he had it' (p. 94); 'he had a lot of gumption ... I hated that' (pp. 93–4)). Fred, who at one stage denies all knowledge of the missing sailor, later claims that he 'knew him *very* well ... *very* well' (p. 110). The contradiction, the non sequitur and the incomplete accounts which constitute their conversations merely underline the incoherence of their experience. There are moments of intimacy: Joe admits to a childhood ambition to be a ballet dancer and confesses to his suicidal tendencies. Each character is capable of offering tenderness, but the gesture is never sustained. The rhythm of the play – brief scenes usually between two people – matches the rhythm of their lives. Conversation itself devolves into parallel monologues. Their marriages are broken, their emotional selves distorted. On occasion even the presence of two people seems threatening. Thus Fred speaks to himself alone by the ship's rail. The ship moves on; their lives do not. Only in their stories is there any energy, form or logic; but these conform to the models they have derived from the media. They live at second hand, registering a growing sense of desperation but unable or unwilling to share anything but their evasions.

Lakeboat is not without its weaknesses. A young student, who appears in the first scene and, standing outside the action, seems to imply another dimension of possibility, slips out of the play and is anyway dramatically inconsistent. The character of Joe is unable to sustain the language he is given. After an initial gesture, in which the audience is addressed directly, the device is abruptly abandoned beyond a suggestion that, immobile in a theatre watching inaction on the stage, they perhaps share something with the characters they observe.

Yet even in this early work his central concerns are apparent: the sense of fiction as evasion and fiction as truth, a social world deprived of transcendence, an absurdity to be held at bay by the imagination or succumbed to in a collapse of will on the private and public levels. The very structure of *Lakeboat* implies a discontinuity which becomes a basic characteristic of the figures he creates, a fragmentation which is presented as social fact (a sense of alienation bred out of American myths of competitive capitalism), psychological reality (men and women divorced equally from one another and their own sexuality) and historical truth (they are cut off from a sense of the past). The gap between language and experience suggests a discrepancy which is the source of their pain, and this they attempt to bridge by theatricalizing their world, by redirecting their energy into pure invention. That is both the theme and the theatrical process at the heart of *Lakeboat*, as it is of another early play, a work which marked the real beginning of his public career.

*

Duck Variations (the idea for which came 'from listening to a lot of old Jewish men all my life, particularly my grandfather'), first produced by the St Nicholas Theatre Company at

Goddard College in 1972, is, Mamet insists, ' a very simple play', but that simplicity is misleading. Two old men, Emil Varec and George S. Aronovitz, sit on a bench in a park 'on the edge of a Big City on a Lake' on an Easter afternoon. They pass the time in seemingly meaningless conversation, but their real anxieties and fears are revealed less by what they say than by what they studiously avoid saying. This is a play about death in which its inevitability and immediate possibility have to be kept at arm's length. Very little happens on the stage, just as very little appears to have happened in their lives. By contrast, Edward Albee's *The Zoo Story*, a not too distant influence, seems positively melodramatic. For Mamet, character is action, and the evasive strategies of Emil and George a primary concern. Peter, the middle-class, middle-brow cipher in Albee's play, resists the dangerous business of communication by feigning incomprehension, by putting his hands over his ears and, finally, by fighting for his isolation (a defence of his lonely, uncommitted existence which ironically forces him to the point of human contact). The ageing figures in *Duck Variations* seek to contain their fears through narrative – a process that fascinates Mamet, who has always been interested in fable and myth for precisely this reason. So, rather like *Squirrels* (1974), a comedy about two hack writers creating a script, this play is concerned to foreground the nature of fiction-making; this leads him in the direction of paradox, for just as his characters use anecdote, story and fiction to give a shape to their lives, and sidestep their own fear of death which retrospectively threatens to destroy that shape, so the writer's fictions potentially do likewise. This, of course, is precisely the paradox which creates something of the tension in Beckett's work, and George and Emil are reminiscent of Vladimir and Estragon in *Waiting for Godot*; where Mamet differs from Beckett is that he chooses to locate his characters in a recognizable social environment. He differs from Albee in that, in *The Zoo Story*, Albee invokes the possibility of redemptive action, the possibility of his characters sufficiently abstracting themselves from their situation in order to identify the necessity for change, while Mamet rarely permits his characters such a level of self-consciousness: redemption is not so easily won. *The Zoo Story* and *Duck Variations* take place at Easter. For Albee, this provides the context for a resurrection of human values; for Mamet, it is the source of a certain irony. Redemption is not impossible, but it does not lie in a sudden insight to be won in extremis; it is generated by the imagination.

George and Emil maintain a constant and apparently meaningless chatter in order to avoid the silence they fear. Though their setting is plainly Chicago on a spring day, the sprinkling of capital letters which Mamet uses in his stage directions ('A Park on the edge of a Big City on a Lake. An afternoon around Easter') suggests something other than a realistic setting. The two old men are on the edge of more than a city and a lake; they are faced with their own irrelevance, and their potential end. Their only resource lies in conversation, in the world as they re-create it. But the ironies of the situation are reflected on a linguistic level. The cadences and rhythms of their speech imply a harmony and a coherence to their experience which the words deny. The logic of narrative is to move towards a conclusion (all true stories if continued far enough end in death, remarked Hemingway), but conclusion is what they specifically wish to avoid. It is simply too painful and relevant a subject: so they opt for discontinuity. Yet the pull of narrative is too powerful, and by degrees the fictions they invent underline rather than negate their circumstances.

The play is organized around fourteen 'variations' (on the theme of loss, decline and death), and the musical analogy is deliberate. Mamet had studied piano as a child and was, for a time, a student of dance (the dancer and choreographer Mark Rider was a teacher at Goddard College). His work is distinguished by what is indeed almost a musical concern for tone, pitch and rhythm and a fascination with the harmonics of speech. Certainly, for the characters in *Duck Variations*, sense is subordinate to the rhythms of relationship and the reassurance to be found in the simple sound of the human voice. As Mamet has remarked of his work, 'Rhythm and action are the same ... words are reduced to the sound and rhythm much more than to the verbal content.'[13]

The two men sit watching the lake, constructing stories out of the simple things that they see. A glimpse of a boat leads them to people it, inventing details of those they imaginatively place on board. The sight of a duck precipitates a discussion of its life-cycle, an innocent enough distraction until the simple logic of their own invention leads them to the very fact of death which they had thought to avoid. George is patently uneasy with such a finality, even applied to an invented duck. It has to be qualified, softened:

> EMIL. He dies.
> GEORGE. One day, yes. He dies. He gets lost . . .
> EMIL. And our duck moves up.
> GEORGE. *He* is now the leader. It is *he* who guides them from one home to the next. They all know the way. Each of them has it in him to know when the time is to move . . . But *he* . . . He will be in charge until . . .
> EMIL. Yes.
> GEORGE. Just like the other one . . .
> EMIL. There's no shame in that.
> GEORGE. Just like the previous duck . . .
> EMIL. It happened to *him*, it's got to happen to *him*.
> GEORGE. The time comes to step down.
> EMIL. He dies.
> GEORGE. He dies, he leaves . . . something. And another duck moves on up. (pp. 80–1)

So, for George, death becomes no more than 'getting lost', 'stepping down', 'leaving', 'something', anything, indeed, but terminating. He seeks consolation in the assurance of race continuity.

In the second variation the death of the duck, which is the victim of its supposed hereditary enemy, the Blue Heron, is made more acceptable and less threatening by their seeing it as part of a chivalric duel, an eternal myth of struggle and defeat which invests the arbitrary with meaning. What is true of the fictions they invent is equally true of the characters. Their conversations amount to an elaborate series of attempts to make sense out of the apparent pointlessness of their own existence – to place themselves inside a plot that guarantees them status, significance and relief from their fear of death. They merely displace their anxieties on to the stories they elaborate, though a growing hysteria begins to penetrate even those fictions as they try, with increasing desperation, to read meaning into everything. So, Emil insists,

> *Nothing* is for Nothing... Everything has got a purpose... Every blessed thing... that lives has got a purpose... Sweat glands... We don't sweat for nothing, you know... It's all got a rhyme and a reason... A purpose and a reason. Even these we, at this time, do not clearly understand... There's nothing you could possibly name that doesn't have a purpose. Don't even bother to try. Don't waste your time... It's all got a purpose. The very fact that you are sitting here right now on this bench has got a purpose. (p. 82)

The analogy is designed to reassure; its effect is the opposite.

By the sixth variation George is able to speak about death; now it is Emil who recoils: 'You upset me... with your talk of nature and the duck and death. Morbid useless talk' (p. 85). Such talk is, indeed, a threat, and though they insist that 'A man needs a friend in this life' (p. 85) the conversations which are their consolation are also threatening in so far as they venture on dangerous ground. Even the park, which is a retreat from their apartments – 'Joyless. Cold concrete... Stuff. Linoleum. Imitation' (p. 87) – becomes a trap because 'I sit Home, I can come to the park. At the park the only place I have to go is here' (p. 87). The park itself, indeed, is not without its horrors. The lake is 'a sewer', and beyond that 'the sea is solid dying wildlife'. The duck is now infected with cancer or 'floating up dead on beaches' (p. 88). Thus the bird, invoked originally as a distraction, as a symbol of continuity and natural order, becomes instead an image of their own plight – trapped in a decaying world and finally dropping out of the sky in 'a flash of feathers and blood', as George and Emil intone the word 'dying' ten times. Yet they remain seemingly unaware of the relevance of this to their own situation, as they are when they describe the ancient Greeks as

> Old. Old men. Incapable of working. Of no use to their society. Just used to watch the birds all day. First Light to Last Light. First Light: Go watch birds. Last Light: Stop watching birds. Go home... Watching each other. Each with something to contribute. That the world might turn another day. (p. 94)

The influence may be Beckett; the idiom is pure Mamet.

The play's humour, as with Pinter's work, derives in large

part from the gap between the mundane nature of the subject matter and the elevated language the characters apply to it. With an uncertain grasp on facts, which they nevertheless assert with total confidence, they misuse words, misapply knowledge and desperately shore up their crumbling world with banalities passed off as philosophy. Beyond that there lies only the protection afforded by the stories they tell or the world of habit into which they retreat. As Beckett says in his essay on Proust, habit functions to 'empty the mystery of its threat';[14] so it proves for Emil and George, whose daily trip to the shore of the lake is a tactic whose very regularity is protection against fear and suffering. As Beckett remarks:

> Of all human plants Habit requires the least fostering, and is the first to appear on the seeming desolation of the most barren rock. The fundamental duty of Habit... consists in a perpetual adjustment and readjustment of our organic sensibility to the conditions of its worlds. Suffering represents the omission of that duty, whether through negligence or inefficiency, and boredom its adequate performance. The pendulum oscillates between these two terms: Suffering ... opens a window on the real.[15]

The real is precisely what George and Emil seek to avoid and boredom is their refuge; it is something they choose.

Beyond them is a world growing daily less comprehensible, and its impersonal menace hides a personal fate which threatens retrospectively to unravel what meaning their lives have accrued. Past and future alike are a threat, reminding them of the fact of decay, the reality of mortality. Hence they steer clear of reminiscence. Their conversations contain no information about themselves, nothing that might prove dangerous through its power to stir regrets, expose unrealized hopes and recall losses. Instead they perform: they are like a vaudeville act, each relying on the other to keep the patter going, to avoid the dangerous silences. The real may cause suffering but, reshaped and displaced into story, it seems less threatening. And the banality of these stories is itself crucial, as is the supposedly factual basis of the information they claim to have derived from unimpeachable sources. As in Pinter's play *The Caretaker* Davies's attempt to pretend to arcane knowledge founders on his real ignorance, thereby exposing his vulnerability, so their imperfect command of facts exposes their lack of control over experience. The important thing is not to challenge one another, but to show solidarity. When they do momentarily clash it is because they have drifted too close to the taboo subject of death. The membrane between story and life has been breached; accordingly, they retreat quickly to cliché as a means of defusing dangerous emotions: 'To help a friend in need is the most that any man can want to do' (p. 86). Emil even shapes his protective banalities into a kind of poem:

> Let 'em go to the Country.
> Nature's playground.
> The Country.
> The Land that Time Forgot.
> Mallards in Formation.
> Individual barnyard noises.
> Horses.
> Rusty Gates.
> An ancient tractor.
> Hay. barley.
> Mushrooms.
> Rye.
> Stuffed full of abundance.
> Enough to feed the nations of the
> World. (p. 87)

The irony is that – like Lucky in *Waiting for Godot* – he cannot sustain even this effort. Asked to repeat a line, all he can come up with is the reductive 'Stuff the nameless . . . It'll come to me' (p. 87). Perhaps it is possible to detect another irony here as well, in so far as the writer too constructs coherent form out of the flux of experience, a form potentially as fragile as Emil's. Certainly some such parallel seems implied by a play in which two old men attempt to suppress their own anxieties through a shared moment, through the comforting rhythms of conversation and through stories which contain and defuse their fears, as they stare blankly out at an audience which could be seen as doing essentially the same thing.

George and Emil are victims (rather as Beckett saw Proust's

'creatures' as being) 'of this predominating condition and circumstance – Time... There is no escape from the hours and the days' (p. 12). Time becomes 'an instrument of death' (p. 35). That they respond with such resilience and unconscious humour is simultaneously evidence of a certain admirable tenacity and a dispiriting irony, a combination familiar from Beckett and Pinter, where, lacking control over situation or experience, characters rely on words to create a factitious world within which they feel momentarily secure. On a more modest scale George and Emil are about the same business, building barricades of language between themselves and a world that alarms them, its own manifest decay paralleling all too closely their own process of decline; this is what Beckett, speaking of Proust's characters, describes as 'this long and desperate and daily resistance before the perpetual exfoliation of personality'.[16] The fragility of the world outside, which can be destabilized simply by the intrusion of the word 'death', is the image of their vulnerability.

In this early brief play, the influences seem clear. The setting recalls Albee; the characters, controlled by language rather than in command of it, are familiar from Pinter; the concern with figures who resist their own irrelevance and who fall naturally into routines (in the double sense of habit and performance) to control and even deny their anxieties reminds us of Beckett. But the voice is already Mamet's, as is the ironic tone and the concern for rhythm. The ironies are not pressed as vigorously as they are by Beckett, the characters not quite as solitary as they seem in Pinter. The work also resists Albee's thrust towards renewal and transcendence. *Duck Variations* was, perhaps, a five-finger exercise, but it was one that indicated clearly enough Mamet's emerging talent.

*

Mamet seems to suggest that fiction-making is a means of evading the real; he also appears to imply, with Beckett, that it is an essential human activity and as such is coeval with life. In Beckett's *Cascando* (1962–3) the voice announces:

> story ... if you could finish it ... you could rest ... you could sleep ... not before ... oh I know ... the ones I've finished ... thousands and one ... all I ever did ... in my life

> ... with my life ... saying to myself ... finish this one ... it's the right one ... then rest ... then sleep ... no more stories ... no more words ... and finished it ... and not the right one ... couldn't rest ... straight away another ...[17]

Compulsive storytelling is equally a fact of Mamet's world and if those stories are not always purely a source of irony, he is seldom unaware of a fundamental ambiguity which infects even those apparently innocent occasions when parents tell stories to children – for barely concealed in such stories are the anxieties of adult life, displaced into fiction where they can apparently be controlled and contained. In *The Woods* (1977) (an account of the tenuous relationship between a man and woman) that story involves loss, separation and even desertion; in *Dark Pony* (1977) – apparently a lyrical work which was reviewed as a touching character study – it simultaneously suggests the necessity for and fragility of consolatory fables.

Dark Pony was produced by Yale Repertory Company in 1977. It is a brief play in which a father, returning home in a car with his daughter, recounts a story about a young Indian called Rain Boy, himself a teller of stories, who, whenever he finds himself in difficulty, is rescued by a wild horse called Dark Pony. It is a familiar litany of danger magically dispelled – so familiar that father and daughter intone certain passages together, the daughter anticipating the reassuring ending even as the story unfolds. Part of the pleasure lies in the sheer narrative, the reassurance contained in its predictability and its comforting rhythms; part lies in the comfort to be derived from anxieties stilled and a threatened anarchy resolved. It is lyrical, set out in verse form in the printed text. To most critics, indeed, it was nothing more than a gentle tone poem: for Mel Gussow it 'communicates a feeling of security and even of sanctuary. This is how a bedtime story should always be told; it comforts the listeners.'[18] He even contrasted it with its companion piece, a one-act play called *Reunion* (first produced a year earlier) in which a father and daughter have been separated by a lifetime of bitterness, betrayal and suffering. Yet that very juxtaposition was potentially the source of irony, exposing, as it does, a central function of storytelling. The essence of the fairy-tale and the bedtime story is to deny the reality of suffering, to insist that there is no genuine human need which is not met, no terror which cannot be neutralized. Anxiety, fear, betrayal and desertion may exist, but only momentarily, only as a preparation for a more complete security. The witch is killed, the deserted child found, the poor given riches, and so on. But, as Scott Fitzgerald remarked of the myths of American capitalism, these are the lies told to children at the doors of log cabins, and the gap between such tales and the terrible realities exposed by *Reunion* are perhaps Mamet's real concern. After all, he has spoken of the audience's similar need for reassurance, for works which deny rather than reveal social and historic realities:

> In this country we only understand plays as dope, whose purpose is anaesthetic, meant to blot out consciousness. . . . Audiences aren't encouraged to differentiate among different sorts of response to a play. A play which doesn't soothe or reinforce certain preconceived notions in an audience . . . simply baffles them.[19]

Dark Pony seems to offer precisely such reassurance, but that reassurance is momentary.

The story concerns an Indian brave – noble, loyal to his family – who is rescued from a threatening wolf pack. It is set at a time 'when wild things roamed the land and long before the White Man came here'. Seen outside the context of history, the Indian can be embraced as a symbol of courage and need. But the sentimentality relies on that act of exclusion. The past, once mythicized, can be claimed more comfortably. Even sanitized like this, however, it still carries a tincture of menace, for the story has another component. Rain Boy's greatness derives from his skills as a fighter, while the father's reference to the red colour of the pony prompts his daughter to liken it to the blood that will occur later in the story. Thus there is a hint of menace on both a private and a public level. And beyond the ironies implicit in the suppressed historical referents (plainly Dark Pony finally offered no protection against the depredations of the white man), and the contrast created between this play and its companion piece, there is a further irony in the father's repetition to himself, at the end of the story, of the Indian boy's cry for help. The obvious truth is that when he cries out to himself, 'Dark Pony, Rain Boy calls to you', whatever the need which prompts the whispered call, it is unlikely to prompt a response: whatever his anxieties, they are unlikely to dissolve as miraculously as Rain Boy's. Even story has lost its power to console beyond the moment of its completion, while those who create the fictions do so out of needs and incompletions of their own.

Reunion, the companion piece to *Dark Pony*, was first produced by the St Nicholas Theatre Company in January 1976, and then performed together with *Dark Pony* both at Yale and then Off-Broadway, in 1979, by the Circle Repertory Company. Perhaps it offers a glimpse of the same father and daughter in later life. At any rate the vast gap of experience expressed in the two plays is potentially a comment both on the apparently innocent deceptions of childhood and the profound self-deceptions of maturity. Carol Mindler, 24 years old, divorced and remarried, comes to visit her ex-alcoholic father after a separation of many years. This is a reunion only in the sense that they re-encounter one another. The intimate relationship of father and daughter is no longer recoverable; they come together out of simple need. Like Rain Boy they are both abandoned, lonely and distraught. But there is no Dark Pony for them; simply another human being whose need precipitates a meeting that contains its own terrors. Time has opened a gulf between them which seems unbridgeable; they are strangers trying to re-create a relationship they fear, for it tells them of their own decline. That double response is apparent from the play's opening lines, in which the father hesitates between banality and truth, failing to recognize a daughter who has changed in more than appearance:

> I would of recognized you anywhere.
> It is you. Isn't it?
> Carol. Is that you? (p. 5)

The former relationship exists only as parody: 'You wanna hear a story?' asks Bernie. 'I'll tell you a story.' But now the story concerns neither security nor sanctuary. Instead he offers an account of a time when he had 'been drunk . . . for several years' and, away on a temporary job, had missed his brother's funeral. It concludes not with a comforting resolution but with his memory of his sister-in-law's comment: 'If I ever catch you in my sight again, drunk or sober, I'm going to punch your fucking heart out' (p. 15). His repeated offer – 'Let me tell you a story' – becomes merely an ironic litany. In fact, his stories combine self-justification with self-pity, when they are not simply offered as means of evading the truth about himself and his daughter, when they are not deployed as a protection against the real meeting of minds which can only threaten his detachment and expose the extent of his failure. He recounts the events of a drunken New Year's Eve for no apparent reason other than to fill in the blanks of the years of separation, and to stave off the embarrassment of facing what they have both become.

The vision of personal relationships conjured up by the play is bleak. Bernie is twice divorced; so is the woman with whom he now contemplates marriage. He has lost contact not only with Carol, herself divorced and remarried, but also with his son by his second wife. His first wife's new husband had himself been divorced, and Carol gets on neither with her new husband nor with the children by his former marriage. No stability exists in human relationships; marriage plainly does nothing to neutralize the loneliness that precipitates it. Bernie's advice to his daughter now is that

> It's a fucking jungle out there. And you got to learn
> the rules because *nobody's* going to learn them for
> you.
> ... Pay the price.
> Always the price. Whatever it is. (pp. 23–4)

The image of society the play presents is the opposite of that implied by the title. As Carol remarks, somewhat redundantly,

> ... Everyone's divorced. Every kid on
> the block's got three sets of parents.
> ... I come from a Broken Home.
> The most important institution in America. (p. 29)

She searches out her father, she explains, because she 'felt lonely'; her father is thinking of marrying again for 'Companionship'; yet neither seems likely to succeed in purging that loneliness.

Here, as elsewhere, Mamet's characters are desperate, appearing to share little beyond their evident need for contact.

Their conversations are, in effect, overlapping monologues. Bernie's choice of a wife suggests little beyond two people drifting together:

> She knows me. I know her.
> I respect her.
> She's a good worker, she knows my past.
> I think she loves me. She's about forty. . . .
> Was married once.
> It's like a habit. (p. 21)

It is, indeed; they marry strangers who can no more offer them what they need than they can offer anything in return. And all the while time is passing: as Bernie says, 'it's about time' (p. 23). There comes a moment at which what once was disappointment, a temporary failure or a frustrated desire becomes something more – a complete account of experience. That is precisely what father and daughter fear; they will have to accept the emptiness of their lives as final and definitional. His assertion that he is 'a happy man now' (p. 22) and her agreement that she has 'a lot of possibilities' (p. 23) are belied by their circumstances and the hints they drop of the profundity of their disillusionment. When Bernie insists on the need to seize happiness, he does so in terms that underline the selfishness that has destroyed his relationships, appropriating the language of commercial aggression to describe mutual fulfilment:

> . . . What have you got to lose?
> Take a chance.
> You got to take your chance for happiness.
> You got to grab it.
> You got to know it and you got to want it.
> And you got to *take* it.
> . . . You wanna drink? Go drink.
> You wanna do *this*?
> Pay the price.
> Always the price. Whatever it is.
> And you gotta know it and be prepared to pay it if you don't want it to pass you by.
> And if you don't know that, you gotta find it out, and that's all I know. (pp. 23–4)

The sad fact is that that really is all he knows. This is the philosophy which has brought him to his lonely apartment, cut off from all those he once believed he cared for, and from whom he had severed himself in a vain search for satisfaction.

His daughter, similarly deprived of love, seems concerned only with what a relationship can offer. Her husband's children are an encumbrance, and he is 'a lousy fuck'. She comes to her father in an attempt to return to the past, to reach back beyond the betrayals and the failures to the time when she had thought of her father as an Indian brave (a conscious echo of *Dark Pony*); he, similarly, retreats into memory, to the only moments in his life which seemed to have any significance to him. 'The only two worthwhile things I ever did in my life', he insists, 'were work for the Phone Company and fire a machine gun' (p. 26), neither of which he can any longer do and neither of which relates to the human relationships that he seeks but fails to value. Though the play ends with an apparent reconciliation, that reunion seems no more likely to transform them than the suggestion that they should visit a church and renew a faith they never had. A reunion implies a former union; of that there is scant evidence.

The characters speak, for the most part, in short, staccato sentences, almost as though it is difficult to sustain a thought or relate one experience to another. Memories seem to come in random order; only the stories that Bernie tells seem genuinely fluent, as events from the past are given narrative shape. Unlike the present relationship, which is fraught with danger, accusations, potential embarrassments and emotional traps, the past, once reshaped by memory and imagination, is an object that can be handled with relative safety. He may claim that the central truth he has learned is that 'you gotta be where you are./ . . . While you're there' (p. 36), but in a sense neither father nor daughter is present. The only place where they can meet with any security is a past protected from knowledge of the betrayals that followed; it is in a fiction. He is to be the trusted father, the faithful Indian protector; she, the child, visiting the Science Museum with her parents. He even proposes just such a visit in a vain attempt to recapture that past. The impossibility of a reunion – equally apparent on a linguistic level, since their private fears and needs fail to coincide even on this plane –

underscores the difference between memory and experience, story and reality. The 'stories' he tells are elaborate exercises in self-justification; the memories he strings together have a poetic quality, partly because of a touching banality which he fails to perceive as such. But while Bernie retreats into words, a spill of narrative thrown out as a barrier against feeling (he has three-quarters of the lines in the play), his daughter speaks more tersely, even monosyllabically. In a sense her desperation is the greater, her resources the less. Carol is 24 years old (the chronology seems a little out of hand, the text informing us that she is 24, her father making her 26, perhaps a sign of his own disregard of others), married for the second time and to a man who no longer sleeps with her, childless, and alienated from her stepchildren. Desperate, she has no one to reach out for but a man who is himself baffled, frightened of real contact.

*

Six years later Mamet returned to the ironies potentially generated by the notion of reunion. *The Disappearance of the Jews* (copyrighted in 1982) brings together two men, Jews, who lament the failure of their lives. It is not that their lives have fallen short of their dreams; they had none. As with so many of Mamet's characters, their aspirations seem to have been limited to a sexual freedom which has proved no more satisfying than their marriages.

Bobby Gould seems on the point of leaving his wife; his companion, Joey Lewis, who is concerned with his physical deterioration no less than his social and economic irrelevance, sees his wife as inhibiting the affairs he wishes he could have. Already the past has become little more than a jumble of half-remembered sexual encounters, while the future means nothing but despair and decline. Life, Joey observes, 'is very short . . . We're sitting on the stoop, we're *old* . . . (*Pause*) We're *married* . . . we have *kids* . . . every night I pray that I can get through life without *murdering* anybody.'[20] They feel no connection between themselves and their situation. As Joey laments, 'Everything, everything, everything . . . it's . . . I'll tell you; it's a mystery, Bob . . . *everything. (Pause)* I don't know how things work . . . And we have no connection' (pp. 40–1). The result is a bitterness they seek to assuage with fantasies in which they see themselves as reclaiming a Jewish identity that has plainly meant little to them. Feeling the need for some sense of ritual, they try to attach themselves to a Jewish experience which they see only from the outside and only in terms they can relate to public notions of economic or physical power.

Bobby fantasizes about the attractions of Hollywood, which he presumes to be controlled by Jews; Joey perversely laments his failure to experience the Holocaust, not because he seeks solidarity with those who suffered but because he feels he would have played a heroic role in the struggle. Rather than act in the present, both fantasize about the past. While Joey insists that 'The only bar between me and what I would like to do is doing it' (p. 38), the truth beneath the confident banality is lost to him.

The play's title seems to suggest not simply loss of identity through assimilation, but, more importantly, that erosion of the self which stems from a denial of history and of the power of the individual to intervene in his own life. The physical inertia of his characters – they never stir from the hotel room in which they meet – underlines the extent to which they have conspired in their own irrelevance. The difference between their empty conversation and that in *Duck Variations* is that now the two men who fill an empty life with fantasies and who regret the pressure of time are only in their late thirties.

*

Mamet pictures a society slowly disintegrating because those who inhabit it have lost any sense of community, any concept of values beyond those offered to them by a competitive capitalism. He is, above all, a poet of loss, and not the least of the ironies of his work is the manner in which the inarticulate sounds made by his characters are themselves shaped into effective harmonies. The seductive rhythms to which his characters are liable to succumb – the rhythms generated by conversations which are more like parallel monologues than genuine exchanges of information or feeling – are equally those of his plays, and the fascinating aspect of his work is the extent to which he acknowledges this and seeks to resist his own coherences. For the most part he achieves this by foregrounding the performatics of his characters, underscoring their retreat into narrative, and identifying the fantasies which come to stand as substitutes for the painful reality of relationship. Seeking reunion – between separate selves, between identity and image – they remain, for the most part, separate, isolated and lonely.

Yet, to locate an analysis of the moral incoherences, the social discontinuities and the linguistic deceits of the private and public worlds in a play which is itself a carefully shaped fiction is potentially to deny the force of the analysis. To acknowledge the distracting and deceptive nature of storytelling through the medium of story is to commit oneself to a tension that involves a high degree of self-consciousness if it is not to devolve into simple contradiction. This is precisely what happens in Mamet's work. He exposes the ambiguity by means of ironic juxtaposition and by seeking to undermine the consonance towards which his stories move. This is, in effect, what he does in *Dark Pony*. The fact that Mamet himself is the child of divorced parents perhaps adds poignancy to this account of a father's attempt to reassure his child that she will not be abandoned; but, beyond this privileged knowledge, the text is sufficiently destabilized by the father's introspection, implying the gap between his experience and that of his daughter, to curdle the convention. Certainly his response to storytelling by his characters is deeply ambiguous in many of his plays, and the narrative logic – which moves from disturbance to reassurance – ironized. *Duck Variations* ends with a flip remark, *Sexual Perversity in Chicago* with a confident tone, *American Buffalo* with a restored relationship, *Dark Pony* with dispelled fears, *Reunion* with renewed hope, and so on; yet in each case there is an ironic undertow. Anxieties have been too carefully exposed, evasions too precisely delineated, loneliness too clearly established to permit so casual a resolution. The rhythm of the play once stilled, what remains is a sense of the wounds that have not been cauterized by simple process and of needs not even perceived for what they are, let alone satisfied.

Still there are moments in his work when the ability to generate fictions, to play roles with conviction and verve, to propose a narrative that acknowledges both the need for reassurance and the mutuality implied by the co-presence of storyteller and listener, suggests that there is more at stake than a simple failure of nerve. If many of his characters merely plunder those fantasies that have been wilfully deployed by a society where myths are no more than the agents of commerce, there are fictions which spill out of other needs. Paul Valéry once remarked that we live only by fictions, by our projects, hopes, memories and regrets. We are, he suggested, in some final sense no more than a perpetual invention. For Mamet, the paramount need is to distinguish between those fictions that acknowledge and in some sense satisfy genuine human needs, and those that deny them.

Mamet writes about characters whose capacity for action is limited. His figures have lost their will to act; the benches they frequent, the rooms they inhabit, and the diminished world of possibility they acknowledge, all define the extent of the freedom they are prepared to grasp. To act – in the sense of realizing one's capacity for action – is to incur risk, to precipitate unknown consequences, to acknowledge responsibility, to suffer effects. So they substitute another kind of acting: simulation, performance, deceit. They retreat from that very social complexity and dynamic action the stage so often dramatizes; and, as a result, language has to bear the principal burden. *Duck Variations*, *Dark Pony* and to an extent *Reunion* and *The Disappearance of the Jews* are, it is true, plays that might be thought to work with almost equal effect on the radio; what would be lost, however, is the contrast between an expansive and sometimes confident language and a manifestly reductive physical setting. It is this juxtaposition which generates part of the effect. The British playwright David Hare has said that theatre is the ideal instrument for exposing the lie, since it can simultaneously present appearance and reality. He offered the remark in defence of his own concern with a socially and politically committed theatre (an element of Mamet's work that intensified throughout the 1970s and early 1980s), but it also underlines that discrepancy between language and situation, word and act, which is always central to Mamet's technique. He requires his audience to listen with a degree of concentration greater than that required to respond to the unravelling of plot and the slow revelation of character.

Character matters here, but it is expressed primarily through fragmenting verbal clues: hesitations, sudden silences, tone, rhythm. Within the apparent harmonics of conversation are dissonances that suddenly expose the extent of alienation, the nature and profundity of personal and social anxieties. The plays exist for those moments. The reassuring worlds which his characters construct prove predictably fragile; the sound of their fracturing provides the background noise against which they enact their lives. Mamet has something of the artist's eye for creating painterly tableaux where realism is subtly deformed, as it is in art by the photorealists whose own portraits of urban vacuity combined realist aesthetics with self-conscious techniques that destabilize the reality they seemed to embrace.

The effectiveness of these plays in the theatre relies almost wholly on the extent to which the cadences, the tonal quality, the lexical disturbances, the rhythmic patterns of Mamet's text are reproduced, rather as a musician responds to a score. That is plainly not simply a matter of verbal precision, since much of the effect is likely to derive from the juxtaposition of the words the actors speak, and the attitude they imply; the contrast is not only between what they say and how they say it but also between relationships implied proxemically (through the physical relationships between the characters on stage) and those implied linguistically. As Beckett and Pinter have shown, theatrical minimalism can gain in intensity what it seems to sacrifice in terms of range of dramatic effect – the characters and set operating with the power of an image where the focus is on the closed world that the characters can escape only through imagination and language.

But despite the fact that Mamet has always been most at ease when exploring the tensions between two characters (even in *American Buffalo* and *Glengarry, Glen Ross* individual scenes tend to isolate two figures), almost as though they constituted a critical mass, as a social critic he resists that kind of minimalism in much of his later work. The stage begins to fill with the details of social living, and the action speeds up as he seeks to capture the sometimes frenetic pulse of urban experience. Where at times his characters reach uncertainly for language, or seek to neutralize an incipient hysteria with words, he is equally aware that the urgent pursuit of experience, on a private or public level, could conceal a terror no less profound for being obscured by a deceptive energy.

3

'SEXUAL PERVERSITY IN CHICAGO', 'THE WOODS'

In none of his plays is the frenetic energy of city life more apparent than in *Sexual Perversity in Chicago*, which was voted best Chicago play of 1974, and, after an Off-Off-Broadway run in 1975, won an Obie award for its Off-Broadway production. A purely original work, it offers a bleak yet brilliantly funny account of sexual relationships in late twentieth-century urban America, this time filling the stage with movement, brief pulses of action. It concerns two men (Dan Shapiro and Bernie Litko), aggressively sexist and sexually predatory (at least on the level of language), and two women (Deborah Solomon and Joan Webber) disposed towards sexual experiment.

In his essay 'The Put-Together Girl', written in the mid-1960s, Tom Wolfe wrote of the vogue for silicone injections among women:

> Carol Doda's doctor on Ocean Avenue in San Francisco has an on-going waiting list of women of all sorts, not showgirls, who want the series of injections. Well, why should any woman *wait* – wait for what? – when the difference between dreariness and *appeal* is just a few centimeters of solid tissue.[21]

Tom Wolfe's woman is 'put together' not so much by herself as by public myths of sexuality; Bernie Litko's model woman is similarly one who disturbs none of his prejudices, makes no demands, does nothing but satisfy what he imagines to be his desires. He recites a reductive litany: 'Tits and Ass. Tits and Ass. Tits and Ass. Tits and Ass. Blah de Bloo. Blah de Bloo. Blah de Bloo' (p. 71). This derisive metonym is his attempt to contain the threat posed by women who can so easily destroy his self-image. He and his friend visit a pornographic cinema and revel in a world composed of nothing more than moments of crude sexual contact exactly because this implies no emotional consequences.

Dan Shapiro is described as an urban male, and Bernie Litko as his 'friend and associate', a phrase that suggests the invasion of personal relationships by commercial values. Bernie sees himself as experienced in the ways of women, a teacher. In the stories he tells he becomes the hero, a macho protagonist in pornographic tales, the total implausibility of which leaves him undisturbed. The play begins with his account of a tryst with a woman whose age he gives variously as 18 or 25, depending on whether the fantasy favours the notion of corrupted innocence or knowing maturity. Eventually settling for the latter, he describes her predilection for making love while wearing a Second World War flak jacket and demanding that he imitate the sound of explosions. As he gets carried away by his own narrative, he creates ever more elaborate sexual fantasies. Despite the pose of macho confidence, there is no evidence that Bernie has ever had a relationship with a woman; we certainly never see him succeed. The more frustrated he is in reality, the more fantastic become his stories, his energy being displaced into invention, brilliant set-pieces, carefully calculated, witty vaudeville acts, where he is simultaneously the suave stud and the victim of sexually avaricious women. The reality is rather different. When he encounters a young woman called Joan – in that symbol of urban alienation, the singles bar – his pitch, a curious blend of condescension, falsehood and aggression, is met by a response no less self-consciously assertive: 'Forgive me if I'm being too personal . . . but I do not find you sexually attractive' (pp. 56–7). His reply expresses not just his own model of personal relationships but that of Madison Avenue and Hollywood, where sexual availability is a constant subtext:

> just who the fuck do you think you are, God's gift to Women? I mean where do you fucking get off with this shit. You don't want to get come on to, go enroll in a convent. You think I don't have better things to do? I don't have better ways to spend my hours than to listen to some nowhere cunt

> try out cute bits on me? I mean why don't you just clean your fucking act up, Missy. You're living in a city in 1976 ... You're a grown woman, behave like it for chrissakes. Huh? I mean, what the fuck do you think society is, just a bunch of rules strung together for your personal pleasure? (p. 57)

His appropriation of the language of civics to justify his actions is a typical Mamet device. Like so many of his other characters, Bernie has absorbed the language but not the reality of American liberal principles.

And language is very much the subject of the play. Mamet has pointed out that 'Voltaire said words were invented to hide feelings', and insisted 'That's what the play is about.'[22] The locker-room familiarity, by which women become 'broads' desperate for sexual favours, determines the way in which Bernie responds to those he meets, while the exaggerated rhetoric of pornography and casual sexism leaves Danny unprepared for a real sexual experience or the pressure of a genuine relationship. When Danny succeeds in seducing Deborah, a young woman in her twenties, the result is predictably anticlimactic. None the less their relationship seems to threaten Bernie, and Deborah's friend Joan, who value only the apparently simple, undemanding and essentially adolescent camaraderie of the same sex. According to Mamet, writing in the *New York Times*, Joan sees men as 'problematical creatures which are necessary to have a relationship with because that's what society says, but it never really works out. It's nothing but a schlep, a misery constantly.'[23] There is, however, more to her lament, for

> there exists the very real possibility that the whole thing is nothing other than a mistake of *rather* large magnitude, and that it never *was* supposed to work out ... trying to fit ourselves to a pattern we can neither *understand* (although we pretend to) nor truly afford to *investigate* (although we pretend to). (p. 67)

Seen thus, the imperfect relationship between men and women seems symptomatic of a more profound failure of perception and understanding, as a possible source of consolation and meaning becomes a cause of alienation, and even evidence of absurdity.

Mamet is a social critic, more so perhaps than his predecessors. He denounces the brutal fiats of capitalism and the demeaning images deployed by its agents, attacks the corruptions and venality of commerce and exposes the alienations generated by urban life, deplores the substitution of artificial for real values, the erosion of human relationships and the decay of a language expressive of genuine human needs. But that social critique suggests something else. The sense of loss that dominates his work is not purely a product of a consumer society in which the values of the market have spilled over into human affairs, nor entirely caused by that sense of isolation bred by urban anonymity – though those forces are powerful enough. It is more fundamental than that. His characters register loss, but lack the language to express or the will to neutralize it. Some resource is no longer available to them; genuine human contact no longer seems credible. In interview, Mamet tends to trace this to its roots in social process; but the plays are less confident. His characters are actors living their lives at second hand. Their attitudes are indeed shaped by the language and the imagery of a manipulative capitalism, but this is because of a terrible vacancy at the heart of their lives. They seem curiously detached from their own experiences, watching their slow drift towards oblivion as if they were powerless to intervene. They lack the words to express their feelings and are terrified of those who share their plight, unwilling to chance the vulnerability which is a product and precondition of relationship. They retreat into fantasy because it has a shape, a coherence and a logic they fail to find in their own lives. Despite the virtually Marxist analysis which he offers of capitalism in a state of decline, Mamet does not suggest that the alienation he identifies and dramatizes can be neutralized by social action: for a writer influenced by Beckett and Pinter such ironies are not so readily dissolved. Indeed, his later play, *The Woods* (1977), suggests that the complex misunderstandings between men and women are more than a product of the crude images and reductive language deployed by the media. The anxieties go deeper; mutuality is more suspect, relationships more problematic. What is missing from his characters' lives is any definable sense of values beyond the material, any clear conception of need unrelated to immediate physical urgencies.

They are, indeed, almost as much victims of their own failure of imagination and will as of a system which readily substitutes commercial for social and moral values. And yet some surviving sense of insufficiency still registers and the space which that implies between aspiration and fulfilment is capable of more than a social interpretation. Indeed social and metaphysical absurdity come close together, though in *American Buffalo* and *Glengarry, Glen Ross* it is perhaps the former which predominates.

David Mamet is concerned with alienation, a state which, as Marx observed, involves more than people's sense of estrangement from the product of their labour:

> What is true of man's relationship to his work, to the product of his work, and to himself, is also true of his relationship to other men, to their labor, and to the objects of their labor . . . each man is alienated from others, and . . . each of the others is likewise alienated from human life.[24]

In the context of such alienation, 'Everyone tries to establish over others an *alien* power in order to find there the satisfaction of his own egoistic need.' Human relations thus come to rest on an exploitation that is not necessarily of itself material but is derived from a world in which exchange value is a primary mechanism. One individual approaches another with a tainted bargain, an offer of relationship now corrupted by the values of the market, saying, in effect, as Marx suggested, 'Dear friend, I will give you what you need, but you know the *conditio sine qua non*. You know what ink you must use in signing yourself over to me. I shall swindle you while providing your enjoyment.' Seen thus, people become commodities, objects; and, as Erich Fromm has suggested, 'This commodity-man knows only one way of relating himself to the world outside, by having it and by consuming (using it). The more alienated he is, the more the sense of having and using constitutes his relationship to the world.'[25] This is essentially the world as Mamet dramatizes it in *Sexual Perversity in Chicago*, *American Buffalo* and *Glengarry, Glen Ross*. His characters deal with people as though they were commodities; their vocabulary is to do with having and using. In the last two plays, they are literal or symbolic businessmen, hucksters for possession;

in the first, they are sexual consumers, and relationships become no more than transactions, expressions of a power relationship.

Sexual Perversity in Chicago paints a bleak portrait of a deeply uncommunal country where the relationship between the sexes has been crudely mythicized. Sexual anxiety all but incapacitates those who feel impelled to enter into relationships which terrify them; the result is a world in which there is no meeting of minds, and sexual hostility crackles through every scene. This, in part, is generated by a denatured language, by the pragmatics of commerce and the myths of a culture which confuses crude sexuality with intimacy; in part it seems to imply an unbridgeable gap between desire and fulfilment, as the American dream is displaced from an economic into a sexual realm. The sexual transaction, indeed, scarcely differs from any other in a culture which places a high value on style, fashion and the fulfilment of personal needs. Emotional commitments are shunned precisely because they constitute a threat to a comfortably adolescent world in which moral responsibility can be disavowed, and one can deny a connection between one's actions and the state of society. It is a play whose own energy and compelling rhythms are seductive in precisely the same way that its characters find the superficial vitality of their urban environment so attractive; and in that sense the audience itself becomes complicit.

Scatological, powered by a neurotic energy, it has the pace of the city – furious, relentless; its style is that of its characters, apparently flip, laid-back and hip. Yet behind the urgent rhythms and the confident personal styles is a void. Children of the sixties, the characters speak casually of sexual conquests and physical intimacy, while being terrified of one another, and bewildered by emotional demands more complex and disturbing than they had imagined, or than public myths had suggested. The play is, as one critic suggested, a kind of disco *Dance of Death*, in which sexual self-doubt turns into simple hostility, and the rituals of adolescence become the models for personal relationships. In a society such as the one Mamet dramatizes, where young boys are molested in cinemas, kindergarten teachers are raped, and children are warned against sexual experimentation by lesbians who pride themselves on their permissiveness, sexual aggression has become a principal expression of psychological and social anxieties.

Sexual Perversity in Chicago consists of a series of fast-paced episodes, separated from one another by revue-style blackouts. In contrast to his earlier work it gains part of its effect on the stage from the sheer speed of its dialogue, as the characters bounce remarks off one another, displaying a random energy which is their substitute for meaning. What they value is style, the hip remark, the quick retort; the fast, almost cinematic intercutting between scenes provides a correlative to this and to the fragmented nature of their lives. No experience can be prolonged beyond the moment, no relationship be anything but a temporary convenience. The wit – and the play is one of Mamet's funniest – is generated partly by characters who wish to avoid serious commitment and partly by the discrepancy between the claims they stake and the goals they achieve. If his earlier plays were static, with the characters frozen into near-immobility, *Sexual Perversity in Chicago* is the reverse. The sheer exuberance is compelling. But the point remains much the same, at least with respect to pace. The vitality is illusory, the energy largely neurotic. His characters end the play as they began it – baffled, insecure, essentially solitary.

*

In *Sexual Perversity in Chicago* men and women respond to one another as objects, translating the need for intimacy into brutal sexuality and being driven apart by the public myths that define their relationships. *The Woods* – a later play (it was first performed in 1977), written, Mamet has explained, 'in a more legato mood' – is an attempt to probe yet deeper into the nature of sexual identity. It sets out to trace the failure of personal relationships to its origins in differing perceptions of experience, differing needs, differing myths of desire and fulfilment.

The play takes place in early autumn, a season that proves an appropriate setting for the relationship between Nick and Ruth which is itself on the turn. They are spending a few days in the countryside, living in a summer house to which they have retreated from what is evidently the stress of the city (though the contrast is more apparent than real, since the pressures that threaten their relationship are internal and the natural world itself is the source of threat as symbol and fact). Once again Mamet presents a conversation piece in which very little appears to happen. Two people discuss their relationship, reminisce and tell seemingly pointless stories. But slowly, and by indirection, he begins to construct an emotional world through which he explores not merely this fragmenting relationship but also the competing drives of men and women drawn to one another but unable to find in that relationship the consolation they seek. The narrative compulsion lies in the gradual revelation of individual psychology, the deepening exploration of a relationship; the dramatic power is generated by a growing sense of hysteria which neither language nor the banalities of social role can finally suppress.

Ruth, profoundly anxious, desperate to provoke commitment without surrendering control, affects a bantering tone. She responds lyrically to her surroundings; her descriptions of the natural world, with which she likes to feel in tune, are even set out in free verse. But her poetry is blunted by Nick's prose. She sees the rain and cold as forming an idyllic backdrop to their relationship, as they wrap up against the weather, 'Like some married couple in a picture' (p. 39); he sees them as representing discomfort and possible threat. She tries to trap him in the rhythms of her language and the tracery of her images. He resists in like manner. But beneath her self-conscious, even pretentious monologue – interrupted only occasionally and monosyllabically by Nick – is a tension apparent in the nervous spill of language, in her insistent image of herself as maternal protector, and in the pattern of loss and threat that underlies her apparently random remarks. Her insistence on the details of nature seems designed to underscore the simple logic of their intimacy, which she sees as wholly in harmony with the natural order, but, in effect, she is creating a fable within which they can live, developing a romantic image against which to locate their relationship.

She tells him that the previous night she had watched over him while he slept amidst the sounds of nature and hints at a possible future intimacy:

You could live up here. Why not?
People could.

> You could live right out in the country.
> I slept so good yesterday. (pp. 2–3)

But that intimacy is yet to be established; 'you' and 'I' have yet to become 'we'. A linguistic distance has still to be maintained; the implicit proposal stays impersonal, as though she were afraid of the consequence of presumption. Moreover, the intimacy for which she yearns also has its terrors. Protection is traded for physical submission, a fact which she can scarcely face even linguistically, referring to 'appetites', then, coyly, 'the liking we have for things', and then 'desire' or 'tastes'. The only way she can reconcile herself to this necessity is by relating it to the natural world ('It all is only things the way they are') and insisting that what is natural must also be beautiful. The problem with the natural world, however, is that in nature 'Nothing lasts', so that nature itself, even at the level of symbol, carries a threat.

Those fears cannot be contained; they break through in the irritating insistence of her chatter, whose very inconsequence hints at the existence of other subjects she would rather not address. In 'Hills Like White Elephants' Ernest Hemingway created a story about a young couple whose relationship is clearly in a state of collapse. No mention is made of either this or an impending abortion. Mamet's play works in much the same way – the spaces in the narrative, the absences, proving critical. Like a person in shock, Ruth tries to control a hysterical impulse through a continuous flood of language much as Hemingway's character, in another of his stories, 'Big Two-Hearted River', had done when he struggled to retain control over his disintegrating mental state through an over-fastidious series of actions which distracted him from his central fears. But, where his fear, successfully controlled at the level of language, bubbles to the surface in a disturbing symbolism of menace and darkness, Ruth's growing alarm, barely contained at the level of language, seeps to the surface in the memories and the images which fill her mind. She speaks in Hemingwayesque short sentences, seemingly incapable of sustaining longer lexical units, as though their complexity would threaten her control. The very intensity of concentration suggests a disturbed psyche. Her debates with herself and with Nick over the precise sounds made by birds, her attempt to reproduce with absolute accuracy the noise she had made while walking through the wrecked boat ('Swssshh. Chhhrssssh. Swwwssshhh.'), imply somebody finding refuge in a bogus precision, feigning interest in a subject tangential to her real anxieties.

Constantly changing the subject, as though wary of developing an image or a narrative, she inadvertently exposes the nature of her fears. She speaks of birds that will abandon their summer habitats, of bears deprived of their lairs; tells of discovering a boat decaying by a lake, and regrets that women have always been left behind by mariners and adventurers. Abandonment, loss and decay are thematic constants. Nick, by contrast, recalls a racoon caught in a trap and resists the notion that they should wear rings and bracelets as a sign of their mutual commitment. For him entrapment is a central fear. Rather as Pinter's characters in *Old Times* sing familiar songs in order to validate their version of the past, so Mamet's characters tell one another stories that encode their desires and fears, thereby asserting their own model of experience. Ruth recalls a story in which two children, lost in the woods, are menaced by bears and wolves because of their failure to understand that they must 'take care of each other, and be very careful not to go too far'; Nick counters with a story – part explanation, part threat – about a man trapped in an abandoned mine who beats his wife on his return. She responds by constructing an idealized portrait of her grandmother's marriage:

> Nothing . . . could separate them.
> She was his. Forever.
> They had made a vow. (p. 48)

The implication is clear: she wants him not just to capitulate but to enter her fictional world.

If Ruth is looking for a romantic commitment, Nick's needs are more directly physical. He tries to shatter her intricate web of romance by launching a sexual assault, a crude assertion of force which undermines her lyricism. Her poetic language suddenly collapses: 'You tore 'em, will you hold on, for chrissake? . . . I'll go inside. I'll get some stuff' (pp. 59–60). The assault fails, its squalid nature emphasized by the physical disgust of both partners (a disgust symbolically displaced on to the mildewed raincoat she is wearing). Momentarily defeated, she can only fall back on a simple, illogical and desperate assertion: 'If you come up here with me, that means you are . . . when you come up here that means you are committed . . . Because I am your guest' (p. 62). The initiative passes to Nick. In the face of her evident need he becomes the dominant partner. When she gives him a gold bracelet inscribed with a declaration of her undying love he rejects it. The relationship seems broken. Her attempts to reconcile herself collapse: 'Nothing lasts forever. (*Pause.*) Don't make me go home. (*Pause.*) I want to live with you' (p. 70). The scene ends on a note of desolation, as she tells yet another story – this time about Martians who have infiltrated mankind, preying on their yearning for intimacy and contact. So powerful is this need that in effect it generates the illusion that it can be satisfied, whereas in fact the loneliness is irremediable. She seems, in other words, to acknowledge a kind of defeat.

But in the third scene there is a radical change of direction; now Nick rather than Ruth seems to need the relationship. For the first time he implies a connection between them ('Do *we* have an aspirin?'), while she resists ('*I* might') (my italics). Perversely, they seem to have exchanged positions. Now it is he who recalls the physical vulnerability of young boys. However, the barrier between them seems absolute. When Ruth recalls their love-making, she sees the moment of mutuality as composed of two separate acts, two moments which are expressions of separate perceptions, as when she remembers the occasion 'When I had you in me the first time. (*Pause.*) When you had me. (*Pause.*)' (p. 91). Sexual intimacy is no longer to be cloaked in sentimentality. She mocks his fear which makes sex a simple antidote to death – 'Fuck me. I don't want to die' – but settles for that; for his part, he now admits to a dream in which he feels gratitude for meeting his ideal woman. Her dreams, it now seems, had been his all along. He, too, had been terrified because 'It gets cold so fast.' He, too, asks himself, 'What is the point?', but has found it possible to settle for this relationship as having the power to neutralize his sense of loss, his growing fear. He becomes the child lost in the forest, the bear wanting to return to its lair. The play ends as the two come together and she begins to recount the story of the lost children and their recovery. They cling together out of necessity rather than full understanding, unable even to voice with any clarity their real needs or aspirations. They are united only by mutual fear; they meet only within the fictions they agree to treat as adequate accounts of the real.

From the very beginning, then, the apparent serenity of the relationship is undermined. She speaks of it as growing organically, but plainly the reverse is true. The fact of decay infiltrates the play at all levels, but it is a decay she wishes to resist. And if she has a final victory of sorts this is because Nick's fear of death and of meaninglessness is more powerful than his fear of lost freedom. The nervous chatter stills. The lexical and grammatic structures simplify until the exchange between Nick and Ruth is like that of a child with its mother:

NICK. Can you stay with me?
RUTH. Come here. Shhhh.
NICK. Can you stay with me?
RUTH. It's going to be all right.
NICK. Please talk to me.
RUTH. It's going to be all right.
NICK. (*Pause*.) Will you talk to me?
RUTH. What shall I say?
NICK. Just talk to me.
   I think I'm going to sleep.
RUTH. You go to sleep now.
NICK. Yes. I have to hear your voice.
RUTH. All right.
NICK. I'm so sleepy. (pp. 101–2)

Plainly what mutuality they do discover turns on just such a dependency. Indeed, adult sexual relationships are presented as attempts to counteract fears which are in essence those of childhood; and it is apparent that Nick no less than Ruth has been under strain. What she had struggled to deal with through words he has tried to contain through silence. For much of the play he speaks little compared to Ruth until, in a sudden paroxysm of violence, he strikes out at her and his hysteria breaks the surface: 'I'm going under,' he shouts, and then, screaming, asks the question that disturbs him most: 'What are we *doing* here? What will *happen* to us? *We* can't know ourselves.' (p. 99). In so far as the relationship with which he had sought to answer such questions has collapsed, he feels threatened by more than the fragility of love. Indeed, he is on the verge of total breakdown, and not the least of Mamet's achievements in the play is to re-create this collapse through subtle dislocations of language, through abnormalities in the structure of speech, and through the eruption of seemingly random but in effect symbolically coherent memories and fantasies. Within the context of this hysteria, the complex of motives which bring men and women together are thrown into stark relief.

Mamet has said of *The Woods* that it asks the question: 'Why don't men and women get along?' It is, he suggests, 'about the yearning to commit yourself, to become less deracinated – or more racinated'. In terms of his own career, it represented his movement towards 'a faith in something or other'.[26] Pressed to say what that faith might be, he added, 'a faith in human nature, perhaps'. It is, he insists, 'about change and regeneration not desolation and decay'. Indeed, he sees it as 'a classical tragedy'.

Despite Nick's psychotic attack on Ruth and the fact that she seemingly rejects his desperate advances, the play does end with her attempt to complete the story begun earlier in the play, to move from anxiety and abandonment to security. Mamet himself has said that 'I think that's the salvation in that play', in so far as Nick, who is 'trying to live in a rational world, is dragged kicking and screaming into some kind of emotional maturity.'[27] Yet here, as elsewhere, he seems more successful in dramatizing the dislocations in social reality and the apparently unbridgeable gulf between people than in identifying the means whereby such dislocations might be transcended. He patently works towards a moment of grace, but this remains little more than a declaration of faith. In interview he points to restored relationships as evidence for the possibility of harmony, but, pressed, he admits that this harmony is more desired than achieved. The plays clear the space for new forms to coalesce, for new relationships to be established, but that space remains a potentiality to be realized beyond the parameters of the drama, perhaps because story can never do more than offer arbitrary models. The self-doubt which seems built into his work creates the necessity for incompletion. Conventional resolutions are to be distrusted precisely because they are constructions of the writer. In the case of *The Woods* the irony seems deeper still, for Ruth and Nick come together only through the mechanism of the story that she relates. Only within the interstices of fiction can they seem to find sufficient remission from time and causality to make common cause against the world and their own separate natures. Struggling to escape the sexual myths which bear so heavily upon them, they resort to pure fiction. But that is the source of an irony which renders the final gesture deeply ambiguous.

*

Mamet's characters feel the need for a system of values just as they do for companionship. As a result they constantly offer secondhand wisdom (usually at odds with their behaviour) and announce the existence of fundamental principles (only to abrogate them when it is convenient to do so). They are aware of loss but seemingly unable to reconstruct the constituent elements of the world which has slipped away from them. They make uncertain gestures towards contact, as though recalling some necessity whose function and meaning have escaped them; but those gestures are never completed. Conscious of absence, they fill the void with fantasies, habit, commercial activity or a protective flow of language; aware of disharmony, they find comfort in the simulated rhythms of urban life. Held in a kind of spiritual and moral suspension, they rely on the substitute logic of event to give movement and progress to their lives. Closing the deal, committing the crime, laying the girl, narrating the story: these imply a dynamic otherwise absent from their experience. Not only do these plans usually come to nothing, but there is an irony in the act of displacement itself; they remain in some fundamental sense baffled, unaware of the origin of their alienation, trapped in a world of immediate sensation or mere illusion. Because of this irony, the drama reviewer Richard Eder's complaints that neither writer nor characters show evidence of sufficient resistance seem particularly misplaced. Eder observes:

in plays where there is little overt action, there must be interior action, a movement of the will in its place. In these plays the characters accept their isolation from each other without real struggle. And there is no movement, no action that breaks out of this isolation, or that even seriously attempts to. The language and the emotions move; and they illustrate a situation, but the situation remains static.[28]

It is a curious objection, in the first place because there is a struggle. As in *The Woods*, Mamet's characters do sense the inadequacy of their lives and feel the necessity to make contact. The problem is that they seem literally demoralized; they find themselves in a context in which their gestures are subverted at point of origin by their own spiritual confusions and by the public forms of a society structured on necessities other than those dictated by human needs. The failure of will that Eder identifies as a structural weakness is, in fact, one of Mamet's principal subjects. You might as well advance the same complaint against Chekhov's Olga, Irina and Marya in *The Three Sisters* (interestingly, in 1985 Mamet was to adapt *The Cherry Orchard* for the Goodman Theatre, and in doing so he was anxious to affirm that play's relevance to a society caught at a moment of crisis). Indeed, the failure of his characters to break out of their isolation and the stasis in which they seem immured is itself a primary fact of their existence, as it is of Beckett's characters, and Eder's comments are no more appropriate to Mamet's work than they would be to Beckett's.

The real risk run by Mamet lies in the sentimental nature of the gesture towards reconstructed relationships that he is tempted to make at the end of his plays. For the most part, the ironies built into character and action obviate this, but he himself is apt to place rather greater pressure on this moment than the plays will bear. And it is in just those plays praised by Richard Eder for finally addressing the need for a transforming imagination and moral resolution that sentimentality becomes a genuine risk. He claims that in *The Woods*, *The Water Engine* and even *Dark Pony* Mamet had 'changed and grown so remarkably' because 'There is action [and] the action is quite simply the action of love', that they 'work upon us emotionally'. None the less, he still raises objections: '*The Woods*, strong as it is, has problems of structure and clarity. The changes are perhaps too exclusively internal; apart from a rainstorm, nothing outside happens to test or stretch the couple. There is some airlessness there.'[29] There is, indeed, and it is precisely that airlessness which defines the world in which they move. What Eder sees as problems of structure and clarity is actually a function of character, social context and metaphysical situation. It is simply not true that nothing external presses upon them; their very retreat to a rural setting, itself alive with a sense of menace and dissolution, is a response to the disruptive, anomic nature of urban life. Since those pressures have in effect been internalized, however, the difference between the social and the psychological has collapsed, so that Nick and Ruth become expressions of the forces they had hoped to resist. The tension between an inner and outer world no longer operates.

In *The Seagull*, Chekhov's Nina criticizes the work of Treplev, an avant-garde dramatist, on the grounds that it contains no 'living characters' and that 'there's hardly any action in your play – just speeches'.[30] Although Chekhov by no means associated himself with Treplev, he had so often been criticized on precisely those grounds that it is hard not to see it as in part a defence of his own work. Thus, when Eder welcomes *The Water Engine* simply to say that 'he has only begun . . . to test his extraordinary command of mood, character and language – poetic and specific – with the real changes and stresses of a plot and external reality',[31] he implies the independence of plot and character and a distinction between internal and external reality which makes little sense in terms of Mamet's work (and little in terms of Chekhov's or Beckett's either).

For it is the essence of Mamet's characters that they have failed to sustain a clear membrane between themselves and their environment. They have lost definition. That is in part because what Eder chooses to call an 'external reality' is itself composed of little more substantial than myths, fantasies, prescriptive roles and fictions. It is precisely the absence of a patent reality (beyond the ominous fact of death) which destabilizes characters who opt for storytelling out of fear of that one irreducible reality which remains an unstated but powerful fact. Demands for plays in which plot becomes central are curiously beside the point when we are dealing with characters whose lives are plotless. The irony is that the pressure which the reviewer plainly feels for something to fill the voids left by Mamet is equally felt by the characters, who also try to generate action as a means of creating a belief in purpose and a sense of the real, and who are no less obsessed by the need for plot than is Eder. The absence of a manifest structure of meaning leads them to presume that it can be generated through the ritual dance of sexual contest, the self-referring systems of commerce or the elaborations of fiction. It is the fact of death, with its threat to unravel meanings, which creates the compulsion for plot. As one of Mamet's characters explains, in a brief play called *All Men Are Whores* (1977):

> Our concept of time is predicated upon our understanding of death.
> Time passes solely because death ends time. . . .
> We are conscious of ourselves, and conscious of the schism in our sexuality.
> And so we perceive time. (*Pause*.) And so we will do anything for some affection.

Or, as another character in the same play observes,

> We know the organism is by no means perfect. We can admit the possibility of some divine control (or absence of control). Of some Much Greater plan, or oversight. We recognize this in the body, we can see the flesh is far from perfect. . . . Should we not, perhaps, retrain ourselves to revel in the sexual act not as the consummation of predestined and regenerate desire, but rather as a two-part affirmation of our need for solace in extremis . . . In a world where nothing works.[32]

This is the essence of the impulse which he explores in both *Sexual Perversity in Chicago* and *The Woods*. In the one it takes the form of satire, as character collapses into role and rhetoric substitutes for action; in the other it is shaped into musical counterpoint, the two voices seeking but never quite achieving harmony.

4

'AMERICAN BUFFALO'

> I think that the old order, whatever that means, the old America is finally finished . . . that the frontier, the commercial drive, the mercantile drive was, in effect, a fad no longer alive.[33]

Mamet emerged on the national scene in the latter half of the 1970s. Politically, America was still coming to terms with Watergate and the Vietnam débâcle. Culturally, the aesthetic and social radicalism of the 1960s had faded. The avant-garde theatre (in the form of Robert Wilson, Richard Foreman and Spalding Gray) seemed concerned to explore individual consciousness, to promote the self as the centre of meaning and experience. Broadway, with its emphasis on private anxieties, ranging from the nature of one's sexual identity to the fear of terminal illness, was scarcely less private in its subject matter. Mamet's work cut a tangent across this. He offered a critique of American society – its capitalist ethos, its increasing privatism, its loss of spiritual meaning and social will – which made him a natural successor to such writers as Arthur Miller, Clifford Odets and Eugene O'Neill. Yet if he, like them, saw the theatre as a moral force he also displayed a contemporary concern for the processes of communication, the degree to which language determines action and fiction the components of the private and public world. In other words, he seemed to be a blend of the old and the new. Much the same could be said of his political position: rejecting the unrestricted individualism of American myth and deploring the corruption of American business, he equally rejected welfare liberalism as destroying initiative and eroding the will to act. His radical analysis of American society turns out to rest on a model of human relationships which is not without its sentimentality and a version of national values which he locates in an uncertain past. But that ambivalence explains something of his attractions as a writer.

As one of his former colleagues has said, Mamet himself is a combination of South Side tough guy and rich kid. He displays the salesman's total confidence in his wares and is prone to the glib reply and the plausible theory. He is, in other words, a little like some of his characters. He is a booster, and that is quite possibly where his sympathy for such figures comes from. He has made it; they, on the whole, have not. As Mamet told the director of a production of *American Buffalo*, Arvin Brown, the petty thieves in that play were all trying to be excellent men, but 'the society hasn't offered them any context to be excellent in'. None the less, he admires them, and that admiration is as vital a fact as is the contempt he expresses for the values to which they subscribe and the culture they exemplify. Drawn to the very characters whose illusions he exposes, he creates plays which acknowledge the ambivalent power of story, as it simultaneously evades crucial truths and reveals a resistant imagination. Recognizing the opposing elements in his culture, he is drawn to both.

The Swedish sociologist Gunnar Myrdal once said of America that it is conservative, but that the traditions it chooses to conserve are liberal. Much the same could be said of David Mamet, who displays the conservatism of a true radical. What is true of his political and moral position is equally true of his aesthetic stance. While in some regards he aligns himself with those post-modern writers who are dedicated to dispensing with or ironizing conventional notions of plot, character and language, he also insists on the attractions of Aristotelian dramatic principles and expresses his admiration for the constructions of the conventional playwright. Much the same could be said of Pinter who, while observing the dramatic unities, has likewise insisted on the importance of silence, the value of a realistic *mise-en-scène* subverted by language and action, the force of precisely delineated speech patterns subtly shaped by the pressure of personal psychology and social fact, and the power of conventional dramatic structures sabotaged by unconventional models of character and distorted rhythms.

Both writers derive their effectiveness from subversion, ostensibly realistic characters being deformed through mannered language or the flattening of perspective so that the very realism of the setting is liable to emphasize the irrealism of those who inhabit it. So it is that while Mamet admires the naturalistic writer, whose concern for the surface density of language and fact located a world reassuringly precise in its psychological and social nature, he is also fascinated by Stockhausen's use of silence, the space between his notes. Mamet's principal notation, indeed, like Pinter's, is the word 'pause', and meaning in his plays seems to exist as much in the threatening aphasia of his characters (or, paradoxically, in the hysterical flood of language which suggests the pressure of the unspoken) as in the language with which they try to place themselves in a social drama which will liberate them from the threat of experience. The conventional and the unconventional coexist, and not simply because that is the basis of his dramatic method, but also because Mamet himself is ambivalently placed. While invoking values that his plays suggest have been compromised, he proposes as a model of communality a theatre thoroughly suffused with the assumptions of capitalism, which he otherwise chooses to see as evidence, if not the cause, of a destructive alienation. He is, in short, a part of the problem which he addresses. But he is acutely aware of this.

Writing of the cultural contradictions of capitalism, Daniel Bell observed:

> Society increasingly becomes a web of consciousness, a form of imagination to be realized as a social construction. But with what rules, and with what moral conceptions? More than ever, without nature or *techne* what can bind men to one another?[34]

This is the world of David Mamet's plays, and Bell's questions are in essence those posed by his drama. Reality, apparently so clearly embodied in stage sets which seem reassuringly mimetic, solidly compacted with the details of social living, is in fact deeply problematic, a series of performances and shifting codes. Those who inhabit it seem to share no common view of themselves or of their relationship to one another. Two-dimensional characters are located in three-dimensional space, and the effect is to stress the loss of the human subject and to dissolve the density of experience. In *The Water Engine* (1977) the characters are confessedly comic-strip figures, actors playing their reductive roles. In *A Life in the Theatre* (1977) they are literally actors as is, at least in intention, one of the figures in *Edmond* (1982). But performance is a central trope in most of his plays. His characters tell stories, perform roles and stage dramas as they seek to win the women, close the deal or simply deny the banality of their experience. Outside those roles they lack both psychological depth and a social history. They are stranded in a world which generates anxiety and alarm and which offers nothing but fantasy to assuage them. They have lost control of their lives. What is real is money, property, objects. Beyond that there lies only uncertainty and threat. Character and identity seem to dissolve into social role precisely because that is fixed, unyielding and hence free of anxiety. They are adrift in a society no longer bound together by shared assumptions; they can relate to one another only through public myths and communicate only through a language drained of human content.

Mamet's is a world of collapsing marriages, attenuated relationships and disintegrating values. The physical world is in a state of decay: lakes are polluted, the countryside characterized by an autumnal dissolution. The city streets are violent and inhabited by petty criminals, pimps and prostitutes. His apartments are stark and uncomforting; his stores littered with detritus; his offices inhabited by crooked lawyers, hypocritical journalists, dishonest salesmen. His characters seem to have lost their human instincts, except for the blind desperation with which they reach out for one another – a gesture, however, which appears doomed to fail. They have surrendered an essential component of their individuality along with their moral sense. Speaking about *American Buffalo*, but with obvious relevance to his other plays, Mamet has remarked on that 'essential part of American consciousness, which is the ability to suspend an ethical sense and adopt instead a popular, accepted mythology and use that to assuage your conscience like everyone else is doing'.[35] The civilization that he pictures seems to be in a state of collapse, the links that once connected individuals to one another and to some sense of transcendent national and metaphysical purpose having been severed. As he has insisted, 'What I write about is what I think is missing from our society. And that's communication on a basic level.'[36] His principal subject, indeed, is loss, and if what concerns him is an absent quality then absence is equally the basis of his aesthetic. The values he celebrates are those most noticeable by their absence. In like manner it is often what is not said, the gesture that is never made or completed, the subject that is never directly broached, which provides the key to his work; as he has progressed as a writer he has eliminated more and more from his texts, if not from the *mise-en-scène* which roots his work in a social world whose very familiarity is the key to its metaphoric no less than its literal meaning.

Capitalism at least offers a model and a vocabulary for human relations, substituting exchange value for personal relations. But, for Mamet, that transaction leaves the individual with the need and the will for contact but without the words to express them, alienated by the very assumptions which offer a structure of relationship without its substance; hence the curiously intransitive nature of the language his characters employ. In several plays Mamet indicates that speeches apparently directed to others are in fact private remarks, never designed to escape the self. Expletives substitute for coherent expression; characters struggle to articulate words and fail to complete simple sentences. They repeatedly resort to nonsense talk ('blah, blah, blah!'), a mocking parody of discourse, or they stutter out thoughts which seem to dissolve as they are expressed. Syntax is broken; grammar is dislocated. The very episodic form of a number of his plays suggests discontinuity, and his characters seem caught in frozen moments. Joseph Frank has spoken of what he calls the spatialization of form, a move from chronological presentation to symbol; time is frozen, focusing attention on elements thrown into relief by the suspension of process. Mamet's characters seem to inhabit just such a world – a world that apparently once had form, once functioned, once offered more than simple survival. Now, however, this exists only vestigially – in the language but not the reality of liberal concern, and in the myths which they enact, myths drained of meaning and corrupted at source.

However naïvely, much of the most interesting theatre of the 1960s celebrated propinquity – either in the form of Dionysian rites or political solidarity. The world which Mamet addresses is bleaker, peopled with lonely individuals who have forgotten how and why contact is achieved. The will to relationship survives, if only because of the depth of anxiety which urges people together, but the social structures have proved less tractable than had been assumed by either Julian Beck (of the Living Theatre) or LeRoi Jones (the black writer who transmuted into the radical dramatist Amiri Baraka). The problem, it seems, lies less in the over-rational social system Beck believed had repressed our physical being, or even in the effete corruptions of a racist society identified by Jones, than with a modern experience in which capitalism compounds a sense of alienation going far beyond class, caste and economic system. For now the real risk is that the collapse of social meaning confirms a fundamental absurdity implicit in the fact of mortality. The mind, the imagination, the will no longer resist the ironies of being; they confirm them. The 1960s dealt in epiphany; in the attenuated realism of Mamet's world, the true risk is apocalypse. With the relationship between people dissolved, with moral values eroded to the point at which no prescription carries authority, and with private and public fantasies replacing a sense of the real, there is no longer anything standing between us and the cataclysm which is simultaneously feared and desired as the logical projection of our anxieties and of our substitution of intensity of feeling for quality of experience.

Mamet is, by instinct, a social dramatist – if by that we mean someone concerned with exposing the myths, the values and the processes of society, with examining the nature of the relationship between private and public worlds. In interviews he has repeatedly spoken of his desire to capture the essence of contemporary experience, even suggesting that 'I'd like to write a really good play sometime. Like O'Neill, Odets, Chekhov, something the way it really is, capture the action of the way things really go.'[37] Fantasizing over the possibility of taking Broadway by storm, he has visualized an audience thanking him for showing them 'how life really is'. All this suggests that he sees himself as a realist offering psychological and social analysis, and there is clearly a sense in which that is true. In 1978 he remarked that one function of the theatre is to come to terms with national psychology: 'In the 70s the theatre is saying that being American is nothing to be ashamed of. But we have to learn how to deal with it. We need to take a look at certain taboo aspects of ourselves.'[38] The responsibility of the theatre, he insisted, is to 'tell us about our national unconscious ... to make our dreams clear'.[39] But, as the inclusion of Chekhov's name in Mamet's list above makes plain, this obligation crosses with other concerns. Moreover, his list is also incomplete: for example, it excludes other major influences on his work. As a student, his models were not the conventional realists but writers whose social and psychological insights were refracted through other urgencies and addressed anxieties which went beyond those generated by a specific social system and psychological type. Those models were Samuel Beckett and Harold Pinter.

The fact is that Mamet combines the instincts of a social dramatist with those of a more metaphysical playwright. Where Pinter steadfastly refuses to ground his work in a specific political environment, or, despite the specificity of social context, a precise national mythology (or did until *One for the Road*), Mamet does concern himself with specifically American values, though the sense of loss and alienation from which his characters suffer is hardly only a product of capitalism or debased national myths. But his social concerns coexist with, among other elements, a fascination with the processes of theatre, a doubt about the ability of language to render experience, and a concern with the ambiguous nature of storytelling.

The America his characters inhabit is shapeless. Its animating principles survive only as a collection of rhetorical pieties drained of all meaning and moral content. Supposed verities have been eroded by time; personal incapacity and incorrigible venality have replaced a perhaps always dubious national dream of existential truth and personal endeavour. Behind this analysis of national anomie, of a people alienated from the language they speak, the principles they supposedly embrace and the fellow citizens they claim as brothers and sisters but fear as enemies, is, however, another, more profound sense of alarm. The loss of moral coherence and the collapse of ultimate sanctions for behaviour suggest a sense of crisis and apocalypse which transcends the merely social, an absurdity inherent in the human situation itself. Socially, his characters find themselves living in a period without transcendence, in which values are no longer certain and there is apparently no point of reference by which to establish a sense of moral equilibrium, no standard of achievement not exposed as contingent. But this suggests a link between Mamet's social and metaphysical concerns; the sense of formlessness which destabilizes them on a social level also threatens them on a metaphysical one. They are performers who have no sense of how their roles relate to a central meaning; they merely continue to perform, playing each moment with intensity and holding at bay questions which could only threaten the sole authenticity they can believe in – their own significance.

As to realism, his concern to capture a sense of contemporary experience and to locate his characters in a recognizable environment suggests a version of his plays which is in many ways misleading. For he is not primarily interested in identifying determinisms or even in rendering a precise portrait of character, language or setting. He deals in deformations, pressing beyond the surface and even beyond a concern for psychological reality. He is interested in the way in which we create the world to which we then submit with every appearance of inevitability. At the very centre of his work is his recognition of a failure of will, imagination and courage. If we are strangers in the world, he implies, it is because we choose to inhabit different and separate worlds in which a terror of vulnerability creates the very alienation we fear. Mamet is aware of the pressure towards realism. As he has observed,

> Most American theatrical workers are in thrall to the idea of *realism*. A very real urge to be truthful, to be *true*, constrains them to judge their efforts and actions against an inchoate standard of *realism*, which is to say, against an immutable but *unspecified* standard of reality.[40]

But therein lies the problem, in so far as the real tends to be rendered into its most immediate and manifest form. Indeed, more than that, 'Realism is death. It is hard, unrewarding work in the service of a master who left long ago. It is the tool of the untalented and afraid.'[41] What he is concerned with, then, is not so much delineating the social and psychological texture of experience as responding to the manner in which the real is constituted − by language, by myth and by the shaping imagination.

For Mamet, a phase in American life is over. The mercantile drive which had underpinned the myth of frontier individualism has lost its energy and sense of purpose. What remains, and what, for the most part, he has chosen to write about, is the residue of that world − not true myth (which brings people together) but fantasy (which separates them), not puritan ethic but pieties, not a language rooted in experience but a rhetoric based on illusion and deceit. He writes about an America enacting its own past with neither confidence nor comprehension. Remnants of that past survive − in appeals to liberal virtues, in encomiums to community and national purpose (no less than in objects from the past) − but they exist now as ironic commentaries on a spiritually depleted present in which the Other is always perceived as a threat, and the only certainties are money, power, and a self that is confidently asserted but empty of meaning and direction. When he writes about the political world − as he does, for example, of El Salvador − it is as a crap game that a gambler cannot bring himself to leave, or as a man who arms himself to stave off the attack he provokes. The distorted logic of private and public betrayal is rooted in a past to which his characters appeal but which they have never understood and which has no existence outside present needs. That had partly been the weakness of much theatre in the 1960s, which likewise saw itself as severed from historical process, offering therapy rather than understanding. If it resisted the institution, it did so in the name of a self and a community which remained uninspected and which, had they been offered for examination, would have resolved themselves into chimeras. Mamet's concern for the institution lies not in the extent to which it can be counterposed to the authentically instinctual, but in his belief that it enables the individual to break a fundamental ethical contract.

*

American Buffalo opened in Chicago in November 1975. It was produced Off-Broadway three months later, and the following year secured a Broadway production starring John Savage, Robert Duval and Kenneth McMillan. Yet, despite winning the New York Drama Critics' Award, it was not unanimously praised, and it closed after only 150 performances – a fact, for Mamet, not unconnected with its theme. It was, after all, an assault on the American business ethic and an assertion of the collapse of morale and morality in America; it offered a bleak portrait of a country where personal relationships had been infiltrated by market values and the ethical basis for private and public action had been eroded. Though ostensibly an account of a group of socially and economically marginal people – petty criminals who operate from a Chicago junkstore – it is according to Mamet,

> about the American ethic of business. I felt angry about business when I wrote the play. Businessmen left it muttering vehemently about its inadequacies and pointlessness. But they weren't really mad because the play was pointless – no one can be forced to sit through an hour-and-a-half of meaningless dialogue – they were angry because the play was about them.[42]

Don Dubrow is the owner of a resale shop, a junkstore piled high with the detritus of America's past – much of it dating back to the Chicago World's Fair of 1933, which celebrated a 'Century of Progress'. He is thus surrounded by the clutter of American history which stands as an ironic commentary on the drama that ensues. Among this testimony to national pieties a customer finds a buffalo-head nickel for which he incautiously offers 80 dollars. Previously unaware of its value, Don insists on 90; but, far from satisfied by his windfall, he is sure that the coin must be more valuable and that he has been exploited. Accordingly, he plans to break into the man's apartment and steal what he presumes must be his collection of coins. The motive is only partly financial; he is mainly concerned with exacting revenge for the imagined slight. Beyond anything else, he feels demeaned by the fact that someone may have taken advantage of him. A financial transaction is no longer a mutually satisfying contract; it is a battle for dominance – and this ethos also invades the world of private relationships.

To assist him in his enterprise he enrolls Bob, a mentally damaged young drug addict whose dependency eliminates him as a threat, and, against his better judgement, Walter Cole, known as Teach, and described, just as Bernie Litko had been in *Sexual Perversity in Chicago*, as a 'friend and associate'. Teach is, in fact, a brutal petty crook whose own sense of vulnerability and paranoia results in profound suspicion of others. Seeing crime as 'business', and business as self-justifying, validating deceit, physical violence and even assault, he regards friendship as little more than a momentary coincidence of interests. The planned robbery never takes place. Rather like the boys who plan to rob a white store-owner in Richard Wright's *Native Son* (also set in Chicago), they are too demoralized, uncertain and intimidated to enact what is no more than a fantasy of action. They lack the intelligence to plan the robbery – their proposed tactics are ludicrously inept – but, more important, they lack the will. The crime is important to them not as reality but as a momentary distraction, an assertion of control over lives that seem to lack direction and meaning, and as an enterprise which for a brief while gives them the semblance of mutuality. That it fails on almost all counts is the source of an irony that goes beyond the social critique which Mamet has himself chosen to emphasize, and demonstrates a central conceit which he derived from Thorstein Veblen, namely, the relationship between the businessman and the lumpenproletariat. As Mamet has remarked, in explanation of his oblique methodology: 'There's really no difference between the *lumpenproletariat* and stockbrokers or corporate lawyers who are the lackey of business [though] . . . part of the American myth is that a difference exists, that at a certain point vicious behaviour becomes laudable.'[43]

Veblen is an important point of reference. In accounting for the emergence of an American leisure class, he described the evolutionary move towards what he called a 'predatory phase of life', when aggression becomes the accredited form of action and 'Booty, trophies of the chase or of the raid, come to be prized as evidence of preeminent force'. It is a period in which 'the obtaining of goods by other methods than seizing comes to be accounted unworthy of man.... The performance of productive work, or employment in personal service, falls under the same odium for the same reason.'[44] Mamet's point seems to be that American society is caught in just such a predatory phase. Don resists the notion that his function may be to serve his customers, objecting of one that 'He comes in here like I'm his fucking doorman' (p. 19). A simple transaction offers no satisfaction. The essence of their lives is the need to come out on top, to take advantage of others.

The same distortion of language occurs with Mamet's characters as Veblen had seen as characterizing his predatory society. Thus Veblen suggests that for those in such a culture the word 'honourable' implies 'the assertion of superior force ... formidable', while 'worthy' means 'prepotent'. Mamet's characters translate free enterprise as total licence and morality as the exercise of an anarchic will. For Teach, Veblen's next stage of development – the growth of free enterprise – scarcely differs from his first; it is, indeed, suffused with its values. As he explains, it is in essence

> The freedom ... of the *Individual* ... To Embark on any Fucking Course that he sees fit ... In order to secure his honest chance to make a profit.... The country's *founded* on this ... Without this we're just savage shitheads in the wilderness.... Sitting around some vicious campfire. (pp. 35–6)

Since this elegant defence of American individualism and the centrality of private property is delivered in justification of his intention to steal a private hoard of money, he neatly accommodates Veblen's 'predatory phase' to one in which men no longer struggle for subsistence but seek to provide 'evidence of the prepotence of the possessor of these goods over other individuals in the community'.[45] Teach's parody of American revolutionary principles – which themselves managed to combine religious piety, political freedom and an untrammelled free enterprise – is not quite the caricature it may appear. The history of American expansionism (domestic and foreign), the growth of private fortunes and the congruence of wealth and power – the process, indeed, whereby the language and principles of Lockean liberalism were successfully accommodated to the reality of inequity, injustice and a socially sanctioned violence – is such that Teach's remarks are not remote from the historical justification advanced by politicians and businessmen. The fact that the object of the robbery is to be a 'buffalo-head' nickel is a reminder of one specific instance of such behaviour: the crimes committed against the Indian and justified in the name of 'progress', the physical move across a continent (an act of dispossession and genocide) being accommodated to and justified by reference to commercial values. If it be objected that Don and Teach's wilful abstention from work disqualifies them from operating as effective images of the American business world, it is worth recalling Veblen's concept of 'conspicuous leisure' whereby social superiority is denoted precisely by such abstention.

Here, as elsewhere, Mamet is fascinated by the way in which language is used to conceal rather than reveal truth. The rhetoric tends to imply the persistence of values systematically abrogated in fact – an issue scarcely irrelevant to a culture that had just witnessed the deceptions of military communiqués from Vietnam and the simple lies of an American president who had sought to cloak his betrayals behind the language of national security and presidential privilege. President Nixon had expropriated the language of patriotism, the football team and the statesman; professional criminals did much the same for the family, private enterprise and friendship. When Joe Bananno, head of one of the five Mafia families, published his self-justifying autobiography, he called it *A Man of Honor*, prefaced it with a quotation from Alfred Lord Tennyson's 'Ulysses' ('That which we are, we are . . . / Made weak by time and fate, but strong in will / To strive, to seek, to find, and not to yield'), regretted the decline of family values and natural morality, and extolled friendship: 'History had already taught us that the greatest avenue of upward mobility was not so much talent – talent was universal – as it was friendship, what Americans call connections.'[46] Mamet's description of Teach as 'friend and associate' underscores precisely this confusion of realms and values. Friendship becomes synonymous with business utility; where a clash occurs it is clear which takes priority. As another Mafia leader remarked of his strangling of a member of his own 'Family', 'it was business . . . just business'.

To Don, business is simply 'People taking *care* of themselves' (p. 9) and friendship a central value until it conflicts with other values. As Teach insists, 'We're talking about money for chrissake, huh? . . . Friendship is friendship, and a wonderful thing, and I am all for it. . . . Okay. But let's just keep . . . the two apart, and maybe we can deal with each other like some human beings' (p. 12). So when, at the end of the play, they suspect Bob of double-crossing them Teach beats him brutally and then rounds on Don: 'You fucking fake. You fuck your friends. You *have* no friends' (p. 47). Friendship, indeed, hardly exists. Momentary alliances are formed, and the importance of relationship is extolled, but when Teach imagines himself to be slighted his response is to insist that 'The only way to teach these people is to kill them' (p. 10).

The world pictured in *American Buffalo* is one in which the pursuit of self-interest is the only remaining certainty. In a society assumed to consist of patrolling police cars, personal insults (real or imagined), urban violence (even one of the putative thieves is mugged) and paranoia, survival is at a premium. A business deal (the sale of a load of pig-iron – presumably stolen) is assumed to be corrupt ('he jewed Ruthie out of that pig iron,' objects Bob; 'That's what business *is*,' replies Don); a game of cards is presumed to be fixed; a friendly exchange is held to be a concealed expression of contempt. Teach carries a gun to protect himself against 'some crazed lunatic' who may have armed himself against the possibility of assault by someone like Teach. Celebrating the virtues of personal relationships, lamenting the decline of values, and deploring the distrust and suspicion which lead people to protect themselves against precisely the violence that they plan, this group of ineffectual robbers stands both as a justification and an image of that decline. Control has slipped away from them. Their fantasies of revenge and their criminal plans are designed to restore that control. But the very ineptitude of those plans (which never move from word to act, despite Don's insistence that 'Action talks and bullshit walks' (p. 7)) and the ludicrously extravagant nature of the planned revenge merely serve to underscore their impotence (a fact also emphasized by the absence of women and the curiously adolescent nature of their fragile camaraderie). The disproportion between their language and their acts, like the disturbing contradictions of thought ('I am calm. I'm just upset'), suggests (rather as does the famous and similar occasion in Beckett's *Waiting for Godot* in which the injunction 'Let's go' is followed by the stage direction 'They do not move') that the gulf between word and deed reflects a more profound dislocation in their experience.

The language of classical liberalism survives. The idea of a social contract to which individuals subscribe in order to preserve individual freedom still registers, at least in the shopworn phrases which both Don and Teach deploy. But such phrases are like the occasional intact buildings in a deserted city. They have lost all meaning. There is no longer a community to which they may relate. The final irony is that they are uttered by those who have been instrumental in eroding their meaning. Just as Joe Bananno hypocritically deplores the fact that 'American values tended to displace kinship relationships with economic relationships' because 'People worshipped money in this country' and 'in the absence of a higher moral code the making of money becomes an unwholesome goal',[47] so Teach — a liar, a thief and a pathologically violent man — laments: 'The Whole Entire World. There is No Law. There is No Right And Wrong. The World Is Lies. There Is No Friendship. Every Fucking Thing. Every God-Forsaken Thing. . . . We all live like the caveman' (pp. 48–9).

The need for some kind of rules is apparent. Teach constantly seeks to make distinctions that will justify his actions. However, not merely are these rules totally arbitrary; they are subject to constant change. The old principles are apparently as irrelevant as the junk with which the store is cluttered. They have lost their utility, like the macabre instrument that Teach finds, which had once been used for draining the blood out of pigs. Some ultimate sanction has gone, and even the agreed codes which once substituted for absolute authority are in a state of decay; but that decline of values is not fortuitous. Mamet seems to believe, with the early twentieth-century sociologist E. A. Ross (quoted by Veblen), that it is in fact business which sanctions greed, frees the exploiter from guilt and argues for the abolition of restraint. Imagining himself to be naturally conservative, the businessman in fact attacks the very foundation of that conservatism. It is not without interest, then, that Mamet turned to Veblen for his justification. Thus he has insisted that

> As Thorstein Veblen says, the behaviour on this level, in the lumpenproletariat, the delinquent class, and the behaviour on the highest levels of society, in the most rarefied atmosphere of the board room and the most rarefied atmospheres of the leisure class, is exactly identical. The people who create nothing, the people who do nothing, the people who have all sorts of myths at their disposal to justify themselves and their predators ... they steal from us. They rob the country spiritually and they grab the country financially.[48]

If Mamet lacks the pessimism of Mark Twain in 'The Man Who Corrupted Hadleyburg', there is something of Twain's *The Gilded Age* about both *American Buffalo* and *Glengarry, Glen Ross*, at least in his sense of a corrupting venality. In a way he is the poet of a new Gilded Age, but one in which the self-justifying cant of the rich has filtered down through the system. In that respect, at least, the 1970s and 1980s are somewhat akin to the 1870s and 1880s. In *Glengarry, Glen Ross*, a century on, the real-estate swindles of Charles Dickens's *Martin Chuzzlewit* continue, with theft still justified as business enterprise. All that has changed is that these values now seem universal. Where Veblen had insisted that the wealthy accumulated property largely by 'force and fraud', now that principle seems to have acquired the status of universal law.

Veblen tended to use the word 'undertaker' as a virtual synonym for 'capitalist', seeing capitalist enterprise as a kind of self-annihilating dance of death in which mutual exploitation breeds mutual suspicion. *American Buffalo* seems to accept both the analysis and the image. The dominant symbols are those of decay, absence, loss, violence, fear and anxiety. Each character rightly regards the other as a threat. Lamenting the decline of trust, they plan a robbery; regretting the decay of friendship, they plot against and decry one another; alarmed at the collapse of social order, they arm themselves and accept no morality beyond the satisfaction of their own desires. Like Tennessee Williams's *Red Devil Battery Sign*, *American*

Buffalo offers an apocalyptic vision of a self-destructing culture.

At the heart of the play is a coin – Marx's 'universal equivalent'. As Alfred Sohn-Rethel has observed, in an explanation of the principle of commodity exchange:

> The principle . . . taints the relationship of each party to the objects they exchange. For the interest of each is his own interest and not that of the other; similarly the way each one conceives of his interest is his own, the needs, feelings, thoughts that are involved on both sides are polarized on *whose* they are. A piece of bread that another person eats does not feed me.[49]

Much the same thought seems to lie behind *American Buffalo*. When Teach takes a piece of toast from a friend's plate it is seen as an infringement of rights. Every personal exchange, indeed, is seen in terms of its commercial utility. In *The Decline of the West* Oswald Spengler spoke of a period in which power and money dominate and the 'human masses . . . are wafted dunes' in vast cities, a fact which results in the destruction of 'the old orders of the Culture'. The consequence is a resurgence of anarchy in which the strongest win: 'If in the world of truths it is *proof* that decides all, in that of facts it is success. Success means that one being triumphs over the others.'[50] *American Buffalo* turns on the planned theft of a coin – a central image not only to Marx but also to Spengler, who identified a stage of civilization 'at which tradition and personality have lost their immediate effectiveness, and every idea, to be actualized, has to be put in terms of money'.[51] The classical society which he chose to exemplify this was Carthage; the modern one was America. David Mamet assumes no less.

Among the goods in Don's store are memorabilia from the Chicago World's Fair of 1933, which the inarticulate Teach refers to as 'the thing'. When Don insists that these objects are now fashionable and that anyone wanting to buy them would have to pay 15 dollars, Teach replies, 'A bunch of fucking thieves.' Logically the comment should apply to Don, who is charging extravagant amounts for objects which were once commonplace, but in fact Teach seems to be referring to those who buy the objects (or possibly to those who had originally manufactured and bought them). In other words there appears to be a moral inversion in Teach's apparent non sequitur. What he chiefly regrets is that he himself had not 'kept the stuff I threw out' (p. 14). Thus the man who had paid 90 dollars for the buffalo-head nickel is later described by Teach as having stolen it. Similarly, Teach, having expressed the fear that Fletcher, an absent member of the gang, may betray them by performing the robbery himself ('He would. He is an animal'), immediately proposes that they do the same themselves ('Let us go and take what's ours') (p. 36)). By way of justification, he cites the betrayal of Bobby which they have already perpetrated.

Teach is prone to a vocabulary at odds with his situation ('What am I doing demeaning myself . . . I'm coming in here to efface myself'). He sees himself as a philosopher; defending his logical absurdities by a specious abstraction ('Man is a creature of habits. Man does not change his habits overnight . . . And if he does, he has a very good reason' (p. 38)). Language is all he has to conceal the reality of his own incapacities and fears. Under pressure even this collapses into bathetic obscenity ('you shithead . . . I'll kick your fucking head in . . . You twerp' (p. 39)). Finally, manœuvred into an impossible position, even language fails him and he begins to sing softly to himself, much as Stanley, prompted by McCann, nervously whistles 'The Mountains of Mourne' in Pinter's *The Birthday Party*. But if language is a defence it is also a weapon. It is used to denigrate, to insinuate, to abuse, to denounce. Teach constructs an alternative reality as he braids together scattered incidents until they form a paranoid narrative which has its own compulsions. Once that narrative has established its authority, it becomes the basis for action. So, having convinced himself and Don that the baffled Bobby is an agent of an elaborate but vague conspiracy which threatens their interest, he feels justified in unleashing a furious spasm of violence (again, social observation combines disturbingly with political prophecy). When that 'story' is undermined by events, he begins to construct another, distancing himself from the consequences of his own actions. Thus, having wrecked the store, Teach complains of the disorder and suggests to Don that he 'should clean this place up' (p. 50), attributing the anarchy he has unleashed to simple carelessness. If there is a level on which their manifest need generates real concern, for the most part this is rigorously suppressed or concealed on the grounds that it implies a dangerous vulnerability, since, in the linguistic currency of their world, humanity and compassion are seen as weakness, and weakness is despised as effeminate and dangerous.

This is a world of inverted values. Teach, in particular, invokes moral principles in order to justify his own rapacity. He carries a gun in preparation for the robbery in case some 'crazed lunatic' should regard the theft of his property and an assault on his person as being 'an invasion of his personal domain'. After all, as he points out, 'Guys go nuts . . . Public *officials* . . . *Axe* murderers.' But the yoking of public officials and axe murderers, an unconscious irony on Teach's part, perhaps hints at another level of significance. For he explains that he carries a gun for 'deterrence', lest, 'God forbid, something inevitable occurs and the choice is . . . either him or us.' Possession of the weapon is necessary 'Because of the way *things* are'. It is, he insists, for 'protection', and is carried 'Merely as a deterrent' (p. 41). It is not hard to see a parallel between this rationalization and that advanced for nuclear deterrence; seen thus, the spasm of violence with which the play concludes is not without its exemplary force. The play, in fact, ends with Teach beating Don's junkie friend and then himself being attacked by Don before wrecking the entire store, using, as his weapon, the implement once used to drain blood from dead pigs. Amidst the wreckage of the store, carrying the wounds that they themselves have inflicted, they can do nothing but cling together and insist on the reality and utility of the very human relationships they have just betrayed. Teach's ironic lament over the collapse of law and morality to the point at which 'We all live like the cavemen' and 'There's nothing out there' thus has a chilling force which takes the play beyond a simple critique of American capitalism. It becomes a comment on geo-politics.

Apocalypse becomes a natural consequence of historical process. Teach admires the wisdom of the police, who are sensible enough to go 'Armed to the hilt' with 'Sticks, Mace, knives . . . who knows *what* the fuck they got', because 'They have the right idea'. For him this assortment of weaponry is a final defence against anarchy, for without such a deterrence 'Social customs break down, next thing *everybody's* lying in the gutter' (p. 41). Oblivious to the fact that, as a part of the process of competitive armament, he is contributing to the very process he deplores, he coolly moralizes about the defence of civilized values while conspiring to abrogate them. For a play whose première followed the conclusion of the Vietnam war by only a few months and was performed in the context of an intensifying Cold War atmosphere, this dimension of the play had an evident significance.

*

American Buffalo tended to be seen as a naturalistic account of American low life. Praised by some critics for the skill with which he reproduced the language of the streets, Mamet was attacked by others for much the same reason. Brendan Gill found it 'a curiously offensive piece of writing', partly because of the obscene language which none the less aspired to a level of eloquence it neither merited nor achieved, partly because a work in which 'characters of low intelligence and alley-cat morals exchange tiresome small talk for a couple of hours', in order to demonstrate the message that life, 'rotten as it is, is all we have', contributes nothing that cannot be learned 'from reading the papers and watching TV'.[52] For Gordon Rogoff, likewise, Mamet, having listened to 'America's lower class', demonstrates nothing beyond the fact that those living on the underside of American life 'speak of macho frustrations almost entirely in four letter words'.[53] Worse than that, the play had no plot. The responses were interesting in so far as they seemed determined to accommodate Mamet to a model of drama which was largely irrelevant to his concerns. Language, character and plot no longer operate in quite the way that Gill and Rogoff imply, nor is Mamet the simple realist they wish to make him. The fact is that the play's dialogue is far from being a literal transcription of speech; it captures the essence of a recognizable urban aphasia but does so in a language pressed beyond simple realism. The characters may have been based on those Mamet knew from poker games in a genuine Chicago junkstore, but what interested him was not a simple presentation of authentic behaviour. As he has said, 'Wherever two people have to do something they make up rules to meet just that situation, rules that will not bind them on future occasions.' What concerned him in *American Buffalo* was 'What are the boundaries, the rules of behavior' when 'Law is chimerical. Rules are anarchistic.'[54] Nor is Mamet incapable of devising adequate plots; it is simply that he has chosen to dramatize a world in which plot itself – in the sense of an elaborate system of meaning into which individual characters fit – is no longer credible. The very relativity of values, the fanciful and arbitrary nature of laws, invented and reinvented for the moment, puts a pressure on character beyond that which turned the protagonist of the naturalistic novel into mere evidence of environmental or hereditary determinism. In this world survival is at a premium, but there are no characters capable of adapting to that necessity. The need for structure and purpose survives in the futile schemes they devise, as the need for values is expressed by the half-remembered pieties they utter; but they have no resources. Arthur Miller's characters are culpable because they have abrogated values that are still operative. Personal guilt and social betrayal are thus causally linked. In *American Buffalo* there are no longer any values that survive the moment; hence there is no responsibility to be denied and no redemption to be claimed. His characters, like Beckett's, are stranded in an endlessly prolonged present, and the sight of a group of marginal figures filling their silence with sound and choosing to deny the evident irony of their situation is by now an entirely familiar one – though not one, evidently, recognized by Brendan Gill and Gordon Rogoff.

American Buffalo is no more simply about a group of petty criminals than *Waiting for Godot* is about tramps. Nor is it merely a displaced account of commercial rapacity. Its central concern is with the erosion of intimacy, a sense of loss so complete that even the momentary co-operation necessitated by crime, business or a shared fantasy seems preferable to isolation. The impulse towards connectiveness still survives. His characters feel the need for relationships, but seem incapable of sustaining them. They exist in an environment in which compassion is seen as weakness and friendship merely a temporary congruence of interests. Public myths and rituals enforce social roles which seem to militate against genuine human contact. Other people are seen as potential rivals or threats. They are like animals, constantly alive to the possibility of danger. Affection can change to suspicion at a moment's notice. There is a neurotic tension, a nervous energy which is a substitute for vitality. Wary of possible betrayal, the characters never allow themselves to be placed in a position of disadvantage. Self-protection becomes a basic rule and the price is a fundamental isolation. Thus, while Don is patently humane and even sentimental in his relationship with Bob, he is prepared to sanction an almost lethal assault on him. While he professes friendship for Teach, he beats him systematically. The store acts as a communal refuge against the violence beyond its doors, but in fact the violence and suspicion have already penetrated. And although the play appears to end with a gesture of reconciliation – the simplified dialogue suggesting that deceit and treachery may have been temporarily laid aside – it is difficult to credit this with much substance, given the moral inversions of the world they inhabit. Don, though not doubting the integrity of his friends in their nightly card games, automatically assumes malice on the part of others. Teach makes no such distinction, seeing such malice everywhere and favouring the pre-emptive strike. Bobby alone seems immune to this. A drug addict, and apparently also mentally subnormal, he lacks equally the intelligence and the paranoia that seem to accompany it, though even he practises defensive deceits of precisely the kind which serve to erode relationships. Yet, in a sense, they form a kind of family. Don plays the role of father to Bobby, while even the ironically named Teacher – whose lessons in morality are absurdly hypocritical – relies on the very relationships he fears. That, finally, is the irony of their situation.

The reviews were, as Mamet put it, 'mixed to mixed'. He has come to feel that this was perhaps because the play was 'too real', that 'you can say anything you want in the American theatre as long as you don't mean it.' *American Buffalo*, he insisted, was 'very heartfelt' in both the writing and the acting: 'They weren't and I wasn't doing a play about other people. We were all doing a play about ourselves.'[55] Rejecting the view that it is a naturalistic study, he stressed the stylization of language and its strict rhythms. Indeed, the play, like many of

Mamet's, is written in a form of free verse. Like Arthur Miller, who also tends, initially, to write his plays in verse (including, for example, *The Crucible*), he does so in order to capture precise rhythms and establish an ordering principle. He is less concerned with a literal transcription of speech (in which control is sacrificed to verisimilitude) than with retaining control over the harmonics of conversation. Having derived from Stanislavsky the conviction that rhythm is action, that communication often has less to do with words, which may flow against the current of communication, than with a kind of sympathetic pulse, he orchestrates his dialogue according to other principles than a desire simply to catch the cadences of contemporary speech. Critics, however, were misled into seeing the play in naturalistic terms because it had all the trappings of such work – including a decayed environment in which criminals deploy scatological language. But such a view simply made it easier, in Mamet's view, for them to distance themselves from the work, to deny its relevance beyond the immediate world of its own setting. In short, such critics were refusing to accept its claims to metaphorical status. Thus Mamet objected that, while it was perfectly acceptable in Philip Barry's plays for the wealthy to be seen as representative figures;

> in the fifties to do plays about junkies and longshoremen who were understood as a metaphor for ourselves; and in the seventies to present plays about people who were dying of cancer, [the criminal subclass] was not at that time a generally accepted metaphor, so that it was difficult for a lot of people to accept it as a play about ourselves because the convention wasn't current.[56]

However, when the play was revived in 1983, with Al Pacino playing the role of Teach, it received a far more sympathetic and enthusiastic response from critics who now, belatedly, acknowledged it as a classic of the modern American theatre.

5

'THE WATER ENGINE', 'A LIFE IN THE THEATRE'

Chicago has always been important to David Mamet. It was there that he launched his career, and where he continues to stage his plays. He has always been drawn to those turn-of-the-century Chicago writers who had exposed the underside of American rhetoric, while Thorstein Veblen's *The Theory of the Leisure Class* (1899), which draws on Chicago for much of its evidence, has proved an influential text. In 1893 Chicago hosted the World's Columbian Exposition, celebrating the 400th anniversary of Columbus's discovery of America. It was an exhibition which for Henry Adams stood as a symbol of America's industrialization but which, ironically, heralded a severe depression. Forty years later the Century of Progress Exposition played a similar role in similar circumstances. For David Mamet, writing in the context of the Bicentennial celebrations and in the middle of yet another depression, the 1933 Exposition was a compelling image. It is a reference point in *American Buffalo*; it becomes a central image in *The Water Engine*. If his characters exclude history, Mamet does not. Its pressure is apparent in their present condition. They are the residue of a past which has no meaning for them except in terms of discarded objects and a dysfunctional language; but that past and the myths it generated hold a clue to Mamet's own sense of national anomie.

The Water Engine is set in 1933, when, as Mamet has suggested, 'industrialization and spirituality were in the air'. He has maintained that it is 'a play about the American dream and about dreams . . . it is a fable . . . about the common person and the institution.'[57] It becomes an ironic comment on the substance and fate of a national myth, on a supposed 'century of progress', as well as on the forty years that followed; it explores the process of self-invention (a process explored and parodied in *A Life in the Theatre*) and the evident need for animating fictions. *The Water Engine* adroitly accommodates social drama to philosophical enquiry.

Commissioned by Earplay, a venture of National Public Radio, it was first performed in a stage version in 1977. At its heart is a melodrama not untypical of the radio plays of the 1930s, and, indeed, even in the stage version, part of the action takes place in a radio station, as actors perform in front of microphones. The play they enact is one in which individual skill and initiative are destroyed but not defeated by the power of capitalism. A man called Charles Lang invents an engine that will run on water. When he goes to a patents lawyer, instead of protecting his rights that lawyer hands him over into the hands of big business, whose only objective is to suppress such inventions. The law is plainly in league with commerce, and Lang is betrayed. When bribery fails, the villains first kidnap and then torture both Lang and his sister in an attempt to discover the plans. Finally, they kill them, unaware that the plans have already been passed on.

On one level, then, the play is a neat parody of thirties social drama, even in its upbeat conclusion suggesting that capitalism will eventually be overcome by those who combine imagination and courage. But, given its structure, *The Water Engine* is plainly not offered as simple protest theatre. The apparent realism is presented ironically, and Mamet tightens the screw once more. The story of Charles Lang is only part of the play; the radio drama is contained within another fiction. The play is punctuated by the voice of a chain letter (that familiar device whereby riches are promised or disaster threatened to the recipients, depending on whether they send a dollar to the person whose name appears above theirs on an attached list). In order to persuade people to collaborate, the voice recounts a number of exemplary stories which purport to describe the fate of those who failed to co-operate. Since one of these stories is that of Charles Lang, and we thus have a play within a play, this becomes in part a drama about fictionality. As Mamet explained in a note:

In Steven Schachter's productions, in Chicago and New York, many scenes were played on mike, as actors presenting a radio drama, and many scenes were played off mike as in a traditional, realistic play. The result was a third reality, a scenic truth, which dealt with radio not as an electronic convenience, but as an expression of our need to create and to communicate and to explain – much like a chain letter.[58]

So, while apparently creating a simple parable about the betrayal of the American dream, Mamet is also acknowledging the degree to which such parables answer a need for explanations, for plausible fictions, for agreed models of experience. He is, in effect, having his social and philosophic cake and eating it, too. *The Water Engine* does address the collapse of national pieties, the attractions and deficiencies of a dream based on nothing more substantial than possession; it also acknowledges the need for other fictions whose force lies not in their truth but in their utility, their power to offer a reassuring shape to experience, deny discontinuity, neutralize fear and still suspicions of unmeaning. The invention of America thus stands as a parallel to other inventions, not least those of the writer who is saddled with the paradox that the mere act of writing implies the possibility and utility of communication and the existence of form.

The Water Engine is set at a period in which for many people the depression was evidence of the literal and symbolic bankruptcy of capitalism; it was produced in the late seventies when Mamet was himself expressing a similar conviction. It is offered as a critique of materialism and the decay of value and purpose as well as an account of a national myth. The voice of the chain letter becomes that of a salesman for the modern (its mixture of admonition and threat, its vision of a transformed life, being precisely that form of secularized redemption offered by the salesman), but its mad ramblings offer an instructive truth, a truth which otherwise Mamet carefully constructs through a series of ironic juxtapositions. Thus, as Lang is about to be betrayed, a knife grinder passes him in the street, quietly menacing. When the lawyer, representing monopoly interests, threatens Lang and announces his view that America would be 'a paradise on earth' if everyone would only be self-interested, an elevator operator pointedly remarks,

'Down? We're going down' (p. 42). The device is not simply a means of ironizing actions and statements but an assertion of interconnection, of equivalence between public and private experience and between different fictional worlds. When Lang and his sister discuss the fact that lawyers and the forces they serve are 'all thieves', the voice of a radio announcer wishes the audience 'very pleasant dreams' and the chain letter, in voice over, remarks that 'Now we are characters within a dream of industry. Within a dream of toil' (p. 23). And this is the play's clear implication: we are all in a sense trapped within fictions; and the key question thus becomes the nature and effect of those fictions.

As Mamet has said in another context, the theatre itself

> is a national dream life and the theatre keeps the same relationship to the nation that a dream bears to the individual. It is that arena where we deal with those problems which are not susceptible to reason. What's happened to the theatre – which is the dream life of the nation – is that the problems so overwhelm us that we won't remember our dreams, that we will stage and avow and support those things that don't threaten us.[59]

The radio play that he parodies serves such a purpose. Like a bedtime story (like the story told in *Dark Pony*), it implies the ultimate victory of the common man over the institution, and as such leaves the system untouched. Read thus, *The Water Engine* is concerned with fiction in all its guises: national myths of commercial enterprise and imperial strength, private fantasies of sudden fame or humanitarian grace, and the elaborate illusions constructed by the writer which may enlighten or console.

At the centre of these myths is America itself – the supreme fiction. As a speaker in Chicago's Bughouse Square asks:

> What happened to this nation? Or did it ever exist? . . . did it exist with its freedoms and slogans . . . the buntings, the gold-hearted standards, the songs. With Equality, Liberty . . . In the West they plough under wheat. Where is America? I say it does not exist. And I say that it never existed. It was all but a myth. A great dream of avarice . . . The dream of a Gentleman Farmer. (p. 64)

Yet, myth or not, it plainly has a coercive power. As the speaker observes, it is in the name of just such fictions that wars are fought, inquisitions prosecuted and injustices perpetrated, for history has less to do with evident realities than with the stories we invent to terrify or console ourselves. Thus, urged by a heckler to 'Go back to Russia', the soapbox speaker replies: 'Russia is a fiction, friend. She is a bugaboo, invented to distract you from your trouble. There is no Russia, Russia is the bear beneath your bed' (p. 27).

The more people are separated from one another by economic process and industrial advance – the very forces celebrated by the Exposition – the more necessary it becomes to insist upon the possibility of shared experience through national solidarity, utopian visions, the hokum of the chain letter or indeed the reassurances of art. Amidst the squalor of 1930s America, audiences flocked to movies like *Gold Diggers of 1933* and tuned into radio dramas of the kind that Mamet parodies here. That is, they looked to art for consolation, for myths of order, for evidence that the moral law still functioned in this sphere if in no other. The physical realities of life could thus in some way be held at arm's length.

Seen in this way, the fictionalizing process becomes at the very least deeply ambiguous. The man who guides people through the Hall of Sciences observes, accurately enough, that science is 'the greatest force for Good or Evil we possess', but in doing so makes a telling comparison which is not invalidated by his clichés. It is, he suggests, the 'Concrete Poetry of Humankind. Our thoughts, our dreams, our aspirations rendered into practical and useful forms. Our science is our self. What are our tools but wishes?' This is precisely the nexus which fascinates Mamet in *The Water Engine*, for, inevitably, as a writer, he is implicated in the world that he dramatizes. He is a part of that process whereby tangible realities are translated into fictions which are both liberating and coercive. He is also a dream salesman whose transpositions of social experience into art risk offering facile consolation, simple entertainment, as much as acerbic comment, and whose work may be admired for its technical proficiency and aesthetic qualities rather than its truth. He is a part of the culture which, in *American Buffalo*, he had deplored. *The Water Engine*, indeed, is perhaps best read as a gesture of complicity. The very seductiveness of his comic-book narrative underlines the power of the medium in which he works. Nor, as a writer, is he independent of the economic forces that he seems to indict. If it is tempting, in this play, to see the inventor as the artist, whose work is seized and systematically exploited or suppressed, Mamet is also aware of the danger of utopianism, of reducing complex realities to simple pieties. Indeed, the writer in the play – a newspaperman to whom Lang turns in desperation – is himself an ironic figure. An investigative journalist who, half cynically, reminds himself that 'a Free Press is the First defence for liberty', he is equally capable of supplying copy to order, churning out a column in which he promises prosperity just around the corner, and celebrating a mutual trust in which he has no faith and which he is in process of abnegating. If the theatre constitutes the dream life of the nation, it may be in a negative as well as a positive sense.

There is, of course, a fundamental irony in the fact that the central figure of the radio play has invented a device through which he can in effect get something for nothing. As the newspaperman remarks, in one of those ironic juxtapositions by which the play works, it is 'The quintessence of those things which made our country great' (p. 63). Dignified with the language of enterprise and endeavour, it is transposed into a myth of heroic idealism, but the consequence is potentially apocalyptic, though scarcely less so than those other ideals, those comforting myths which can so easily be invoked as justification for violence. Again, Mamet underlines this potential by intercutting between a discussion which Lang has with the abductors of his sister and the words of the speaker in Bughouse Square. For, as the subordination of human to material benefits is enacted, and the 'reality' which lies behind the myths of American freedom is exposed, so the speaker insists that 'we live in the Final Time... With want in the midst of abundance... in the final moments' (pp. 64–5). The radio play ends with a young assistant in a neighbourhood store receiving the plans of Lang's invention. It seems that the battle for good will continue, that all is not lost. But there is an uncomfortable irony. For in another sense it implies that the dream of something for nothing continues: utopian myths still assert their seductive power, and Horatio Alger's fictions of the inevitability of success continue to assert their potent and potentially destructive force.

Meanwhile, the moral dislocations that exist at the level of plot infect the play at the level of language. The barker leading the tour of the Hall of Science suddenly slips into a dislocated reverie about the decay of reality into fiction and the collapse of communality that is evidenced at all levels in a play which identifies differing responses to experience, from political analysis (the speaker), to mysticism (the chain letter), to science (the barker), to purported social observation (the reporter) and fictional transposition. His language begins to show evidence of the collapse that he prophesies. Thus the barker speaks in millenarian terms, locating American experience in the context of other, now decayed, civilizations: 'As we complete our second thousand years' (p. 70). The once coherent shapes of national purpose, moral endeavour, private and public ideals are now reduced to a ragbag of clichés, a few tattered remnants of once animating myths.

> In the delapidated office buildings, and in rooms at Railroad Hotels, in torn and filthy manuscripts misfiled in second-hand bookstores, here rest the vestiges of this and other cultures. Arcane knowledge in transition from the inaccessible to the occult, as we rush on. Technological and Ethical masterpieces decay into folktales.

As the barker asks, in such a world 'Who knows what is true?' His final comment, 'All people are connected' (p. 71), thus becomes an ironic commentary on unlearned lessons rather than the cant of natural unity or the self-justifying mysticism of the chain letter, a desperate article of faith rather than a fact which can be shown to take social form. *The Water Engine* is indeed a fable; but, if its logic is to be accepted, its own coherences must be doubted, as a parable about the decay of form is shaped into an elegant and sophisticated metaphor.

In so far as it becomes the basis for action and the foundation for identity, fiction is not counterposed to the real. That is the essence of the irony. In the world that Mamet dramatizes, the coherences of story are positively preferred to the incompletions and ambiguities of experience. This turns all of his characters into storytellers or performers, who sometimes simply echo the dominant fantasies peddled by commerce, as though they provided some kind of charm against actuality, and sometimes generate their own lives out of an imaginative resistance to the given. Performance is thus offered both as a symptom of a wilful absurdity and as a legitimate and instructive response. If that leaves the theatre itself ambiguously located, then that was a fact he chose to explore in another play produced in the same year – *A Life in the Theatre*. *The Water Engine* derives part of its effect from a theatrical ingenuity in which parody and pastiche hint at the theatre's potential for a purely factitious effect, for reassurance masquerading as radical critique; *A Life in the Theatre* – whose title itself parodies Stanislavsky's autobiography, *My Life in Art* – again, through parody, explores a crucial nexus for a writer who sees himself as simultaneously a social playwright and an admirer of Beckett and Pinter: the link between life as theatre and theatre as life.

*

Describing the difference between writing for film and writing fot the stage (he wrote the screenplay for *The Postman Always Rings Twice* and *The Verdict*), Mamet has said: 'In a movie you're trying to show what the characters did and in a play you're trying to convey what they want. The only tool they have in a play is what they're trying to say.'[60] The emphasis is interesting. In talking of film, he suggests that the struggle is that of the writer attempting to create a cogent plot and a series of dramatic actions and events; in speaking of theatre, his emphasis is on the characters' efforts to communicate, efforts which founder on an imperfect language and the intransitive nature of experience. The theatre itself becomes an image of that dislocation which has been the subject of so many of his plays. As Mamet has reminded us, 'Camus says that the actor is a prime example of the Sisyphean nature of life . . . a life in the theatre need not be an analogue to "life"; it is life.'[61] To act is to exist, to create meaning, and, if that serves to underscore the absence of coherence and sense in the structure of experience itself, it simultaneously places on the imagination the burden of inventing purpose and direction. That process is necessarily an ironic and ambiguous one. On the one hand, it is predicated on the manifest absurdity of the human situation – born, as Beckett has Pozzo say, astride the grave; on the other, the performing self becomes a generator of whatever meaning is available, and the power to invent, as Nietzsche suggested, becomes definitional. Thus, to him, *A Life in the Theatre* is 'a play about the attempt to communicate experience and love in the face of and informed by a knowledge of mortality, the attempt being made by individuals engaged in the art of acting, which is the avowal and the celebration of mortality.'[62] It is, he seems to suggest, necessarily a doomed enterprise, but it is also the only game in town. That ambivalent attitude to the elaboration of fictions is apparent in many of his plays; for the fact is that, while all fictions are equal, some are more equal than others. Conceding a contingent world, he none the less wants to smuggle in a moral imperative. The effort sometimes brings him close to sentimentality when the slightest of gestures has to carry undue weight, to imply the existence of shared values whose necessity he feels, but for whose survival he cannot entirely account. One consequence of this ambivalence is that he tends simultaneously to indict his characters for their delusions and admire them for sustaining them in the face of experience. There is something reminiscent of Scott Fitzgerald in the way he is drawn to the very things he wishes to indict.

Mamet has described the origin of *A Life in the Theatre*:

> I would sit around my father's office in Chicago [and] . . . write scenes on his electric typewriter. I would write them as brief sketches. Over the course of several months I accumulated 15 or 20 scenes about life in the theatre. The scenes were based on anecdote, or composites of anecdotes or observations, and most of them were built around two representative types.[63]

The two representative types are an older actor, apparently secure and willing to induct his partner into the mysteries of the profession, and a brash young man, just launched on his career. Yet each of them is profoundly insecure, as well they might be, for, as their somewhat bizarre repertoire quickly makes clear, they are working in a company which is scarcely at the cutting edge of the American theatre.

The play's epigraph seems to be offered as a comment on the decline of Robert, the older actor, but it could stand as an ironic commentary not only on the declining significance of theatre in the national imagination, but also on the degree to which, actors all, we find ourselves increasingly performing to an empty auditorium:

> We counterfeited once for your disport
> Men's joy and sorrow; but our day has passed.
> We pray you pardon all where we fell short –
> Seeing we were your servants to this last.[64]

Robert's life play is perhaps nearing its end; John's is only just beginning. But, like the players in Tom Stoppard's *Rosencrantz and Guildenstern Are Dead*, they begin to doubt their function and meaning. When they rehearse on an empty stage they do so to perfect their technique and realize their fantasies, but there is a potential irony in the action which is not entirely cauterized by its naturalistic legitimacy.

While acting they live for the moment. They explore the text for hidden meaning (a meaning often patently not there). Once the moment has passed, however, that meaning threatens to dissolve, the careful structures of art being purely contingent. It is a comedy, but there is a pathos that is not purely the product of Robert's declining power. Though the play deploys its own defences against critical analysis (Robert at one stage suggesting, of the banal drama in which he and his partner are performing, that the audience had seen the show on 'another ... plane ... On another level of meaning' (p. 12)), it is tempting to hear an echo of the social criticism of *American Buffalo* (in which the decay of a society was represented by marginal characters unaware of their marginality and creating parodic versions of Platonic myths), and even of Beckett's world of desperate vaudevillians passing the time with old routines while placing their faith in a script long since abandoned as inoperative. Eavesdropping backstage, we are able to detect the artifice behind the apparent order, the unreality of what is projected as real.

At the start of the play Robert presents himself as the accomplished actor, offering advice and patronizing the younger man, who in turn is anxious not to offend. He adopts a pontifical tone, at times elevating the theatre into a kind of arena of moral values and at times collapsing into the pure bathos of professional jealousy, the two levels of discourse becoming hopelessly confused. Thus he remarks of an actress that she has 'No Soul . . . no humanism . . . No formal training . . . No sense of right and wrong' (pp. 18–20), an accusation somewhat undermined by his own response to her lack of 'fellow feeling'. He wishes, he explains, 'to kill the cunt' (p. 19), since she should not 'be allowed to live (not just to *live* . . . but to parade around a stage . . .)' (p. 19). Similarly, when he insists that 'You learn control. Character. A sense of right from wrong', this is not the statement of moral necessities which it appears but a description of the skills that enable him to 'tune her out' (p. 20). Not only are morality and manners hopelessly confused, but the line between performance and reality is eroded.

The play consists of a string of episodes (twenty-six scenes in all) through which Mamet slowly creates a kind of pointillist portrait of the two men. Robert is prim, apparently arrogant and self-confident, but in fact deeply insecure and lonely. The younger man is casual, aware at first of his subordinate position, but also anxious for contact. Despite the fact that their roles are eventually reversed, Robert's age making him increasingly vulnerable, there is a closer relationship between the two men than between most of Mamet's characters. When John leaves a trace of greasepaint on his face, Robert removes it with a tissue moistened with saliva, much as a parent would do, and this level of mutuality is never quite destroyed by the professional jealousies that infect their relationship. But just as the disproportion between their discussions of technique and theory and the reality of the banal plays they perform is the source of irony so, too, is the laboured parallel which they strive to make between the theatre and human life. When Robert speaks of his own life in terms of drama, his words imply progress, his tone a fear of regression:

> You start from the beginning and go through the middle and wind up at the end . . . A little like a play . . . We must not be afraid of process . . . We must not be clowns whose sole desire is to please . . . We must not be afraid to *grow*. We

must support each other, John. This is the wondrous thing *about* the theatre . . . Our history goes as far back as Man's. Our aspirations in the Theatre are much the same as man's. (*Pause.*) (Don't you think?) . . . We *are* society . . . What have we to fear, John, from *phenomena*? (*Pause.*) We are explorers of the soul. (p. 36)

Behind the confident analysis is a nervous appeal; for he is, in fact, plainly terrified of process. Not merely has he accustomed himself to an at times humiliating dependency, but the logic of narrative – beginning, middle, end – carries its own terrors. And if we are to accept a parallel between life and the theatre then the performance which we glimpse in *A Life in the Theatre*, and which ends with the performer in an empty auditorium, drained equally of function and of meaning, suggests an irredeemable banality, and an incorrigible reductiveness to that life which is not, finally, redeemed either by sheer performance or by the interdependence which is apparently a precondition of theatre.

Theoretically committed to art, Robert and John in fact find themselves muddling through ill-written scripts, hampered by the wilful uncooperativeness of their fellow actors, and speaking words that are not their own. If the governing metaphor has any force, human life evidently consists of just such clichéd roles, trite language, mismanaged climaxes and low farce. The gap between aspiration and fulfilment, which seems to typify the theatre, is evidently to be taken as applying with equal force to the life which it sets out to mimic, but for which Robert, influenced by sixties assumptions, sees it acting as model. The need for mutual dependency is clear enough in both worlds, but Robert's ideal of co-operative individuals working together for mutual satisfaction and towards a common goal is, it transpires, no more a reality in the theatre than it is in his life. Egotism and jealousy operate in both. Contact is momentary, alliance a fact of shared situation rather than genuine mutuality.

Disturbed by the thought of unmeaning, Robert is constantly elaborating metaphors which imply coherence but which become more self-evidently nonsensical as the play proceeds. For example a stick of greasepaint becomes a coherent symbol:

> Greasepaint! What is it? Some cream base, some colouring
> ... texture, smell, color ... Analyze it and what have you?
> Meaningless component parts, though one could likely say
> the same for anything ... But mix and package it, affix a
> label, set it on a makeup table ... (p. 65)

Metaphor represents his attempt to cement the pieces of experience together, but his inflated rhetoric has a way of imploding, linguistically into bathos, philosophically into banality.

> The Theatre's a closed society. Constantly abutting
> thoughts, the feelings, the emotions of our colleagues. Sensibilities (*pause*) bodies ... forms evolve. ... One generation
> sows the seeds. It instructs the preceding, that is to say, the
> *following* generation ... from the quality of its actions. Not
> from its discourse, John, no, but organically. (*Pause.*) You
> can learn a lot from keeping your mouth shut. (pp. 66–7)

The linguistic slip and the reductive last sentence, like a muffed line in a play, destroy the whole effect. The rhetoric is plainly top-heavy, as he piles more and more philosophical weight on to a simple image.

> One must speak of these things, John, or we will go the way
> of all society ... Take too much for granted, fall away and
> die. (*Pause.*) On the boards, or in society at large. There must
> be law, there must be a reason, there must be tradition.
> (p. 67)

Through the person of Robert, Mamet seems to be contesting his own mode of representation, challenging the legitimacy of his own procedures as a playwright and even the authority of his central image. For the fact is that performance can be an evasive strategy, and the logic of the theatrical metaphor is no less implacable than that of the life for which it stands or with which it is contiguous.

Beneath the apparent assurance Robert is insecure. He forgets his lines and cuts his wrist with a razor in what seems like an attempted suicide. He talks to himself with an air of desperation intensified by the younger man's evident success. His rhetoric collapses into barely coherent remarks as he laments that 'A life spent in the theatre ... goes so fast' (p. 93).

The metaphor which was to have offered a structure of meaning implies its own rigorous and unrelenting logic, so that the play ends with an absurdist gesture: the actor deprived of audience and hence of purpose offers a benediction to an imagined audience. Scarcely the sentimental gesture which it seems, this marks not only the imminent end of Robert's personal life performance but also the completion of a logic from which the actual audience is scarcely immune: 'The lights dim. Each to his own home. Goodnight. Goodnight. Goodnight' (p. 95). When the audience is dismissed, it is presumably to continue lives characterized precisely by that Chekhov-like ennui, or the clichéd emotional, sexual or social life so effectively parodied in the various scenes enacted by the two actors. *A Life in the Theatre*, in other words, emphasizes the evanescence both of theatre and of life and the cliché that Robert elaborates so self-consciously and ponderously is reinstated and given legitimacy, but not as he would have wished. Robert's experience of the theatre is, indeed, congruent with his life – a series of performed moments more or less competently performed which add up to a completed process. And in the persons of John and Robert the beginning and end of that process are brought ironically together, the younger man's imminent success being undercut by the co-presence of his own future in the form of his fellow actor. Far from creating a sense of order, or giving a sense of structure to psychological, social and metaphysical experience, the metaphor becomes an ironic reminder of the arbitrary shape and contingent meaning of a life performed with ever-decreasing confidence and competence.

As to the audience – ourselves – Mamet seems to imply that we too are manœuvred into playing parts not of our own devising, speaking a language that is not our own, and enacting plots that are all too often distinguished neither by their coherence nor by their grace. But the authority of that metaphor – developed as it is by Robert out of his own insecurities – is perhaps suspect. The theatre is, as Robert remarks, 'part of life'. At times, indeed, it may seem all too accurate a reflection of it, as life turns itself into inferior art. The authority, however, is not yet complete. There are freedoms, privacies and relationships not available to the actor. In this play the distinction is difficult to make, since theatrical and performed self coincide. But in eliminating the space between actor and self it seems to be making a plea for its restoration.

6

THE CULTURE OF NARCISSISM: 'EDMOND'

> The reason that the populace at large is terrified is that the problems seem insoluble. . . . So what we devote our energies to is ourselves and our feelings.[65]

Mamet writes about a society baffled by its own contradictions, a culture with neither historical roots nor present energy. His characters inhabit a world of which they can make little sense, since they are victims as much of their own incomprehension as of any malign force. They can detect no direction, no transcendent purpose, no social or moral contract to which they can subscribe and from which they might derive a sense of their own identity. The only values seem to be those proposed by American capitalism – money, power, sexuality. In short, it is a de-moralized and a demoralized world, a version of what Christopher Lasch, in 1979, chose to call *The Culture of Narcissism* (a book tellingly subtitled *American Life in an Age of Diminishing Expectations*). Like Mamet, Lasch is concerned with creating a portrait of 'the culture of competitive individualism, which in its decadence has carried the logic of individualism to the extreme of a war against all, the pursuit of happiness to the dead end of a narcissistic preoccupation with the self.'[66] *American Buffalo*, *Sexual Perversity in Chicago*, *The Water Engine*, *Edmond* and *Glengarry, Glen Ross* are concerned with no less. When Lasch remarks that the 'new narcissist' is 'haunted not by guilt but by anxiety', he might almost be making a distinction between Arthur Miller's characters and those of David Mamet, for the fact is that guilt has become supererogatory in the world that Mamet describes. Thus, for Lasch, the cultural narcissist has 'sexual attitudes [which] are permissive rather than puritanical, even though his emancipation from ancient taboos brings him no sexual peace.'[67]

Mamet emerged as a writer when America was already showing signs of retreating from that political commitment and engaged art which had in many ways typified the 1960s. In what Tom Wolfe called the 'me' decade, an increasing narcissism was indeed apparent. Self-realization – a concern with individual physical and spiritual well-being – became a central concern. Private rather than public performance, styles rather than issues, became crucial. Sexuality, already proposed as an antidote to a dangerous rationality in the sixties, was now seen by some as a natural form of 'self-actualization,' and one by-product of this sensibility was a social and cultural conservatism – a legitimation of the status quo.

Speaking of the 'new narcissist' Lasch observes that, 'Liberated from the superstitions of the past, he doubts even his own existence',[68] and in a sense this is the starting-point for *Edmond*, which begins with a fortune-teller's diagnosis: 'The world seems to be crumbling around us. You look and you wonder if what you perceive is accurate. And you are unsure what your place is. To what extent you are cause and to what an effect' (p. 16). It is precisely for this reason that the protagonist sets out, like some Raskolnikov, to prove his existence through extremes of experience – sexuality, violence and murder. Turning his back on the competitive world of business, rejecting family ties, he is like Lasch's narcissist:

> Acquisitive in the sense that his cravings have no limits, he does not accumulate goods and provisions against the future, in the manner of the acquisitive individualist of nineteenth-century political economy, but demands immediate gratification, and lives in a state of restless, perpetually unsatisfied desire.[69]

He is, indeed, a purely seventies figure, a kind of parody of the human potential movement which believes that 'the individual will is all powerful and totally determines one's fate'.[70] For a man alarmed that he may be no more than a product of various determinisms, the fortune-teller's suggestion that he is different is seductive, the more so since this seems to justify his subordination of the interests of others. Laying aside a liberalism which he comes to feel has made him a victim of guilt and deprived him of individual will, he asserts his own interests over those around him. The result is sexual and racial arrogance, a reversion to primitivism that he imagines to be therapeutic. Here, again, Lasch is relevant, for he suggests that 'Today Americans . . . having internalized the social restraints by means of which they formerly sought to keep possibility within civilized limits . . . feel themselves overwhelmed by an annihilating boredom.' As a result they long for 'a more vigorous instinctual existence. . . . They cultivate more vivid experiences, seek to beat a sluggish flesh to life, attempt to revive jaded appetites.'[71] The one-time radical Jerry Rubin has said that 'In five years, from 1971 to 1975, I directly experienced est, gestalt therapy, bionergetics, rolfing, massage, jogging, health foods, tai chi, Esalen, hypnotism, modern dance, meditation, Silva Mind Control, Arica, acupuncture, sex therapy, Reichian therapy, and More House.'[72] Edmond attempts a rather narrower and more violent approach to personal liberation, but the impulse is similar. His journey into self-realization, however, proves morally and spiritually regressive.

The play concerns Edmond, a man in his mid-thirties, who decides to leave his wife. He is apparently provoked by nothing more than news of a lamp broken by the family maid, which he takes as final proof of the banality of his life. The ex-communist Paul Zweig once spoke of communism as releasing him 'from the failed rooms and broken vases of a merely private life',[73] and it is release that Edmond seeks, though he has no interest in relating to a wider community. What he sets out to do is plunge into the underworld and explore the sensual pleasures he believes lie outside his bourgeois existence. In an amoral world, quantity and intensity become values, and that is the experience which he imagines to await him – Marcus Aurelius' empire of senses. Mamet has spoken of his distaste for New York and for the contemporary assumption that 'the whole universe is created just for you', that 'no one is accountable for anything' and that 'sexuality is fine'.[74] In this sense Edmond becomes an exemplary figure, laying claim to ultimate experience and finding its illusory and self-destructive nature. He becomes like Büchner's Woyzeck – a man who destroys the only person who might offer him consolation. Believing there to be no constraints on his own freedom of action, he seeks out experience only to discover how much he relies on the survival and reality of the human obligations he began by denying, and how the collapse of moral structure finally threatens his own identity.

Edmond leaves his house in a kind of mock existential quest, in the sense that the French philosopher Gaston Bachelard speaks of the move from house to public world as an image of alienation, the point at which the self becomes distinct from its environment: 'Life begins well, it begins encased, protected, all warmth in the bosom of the house', and the 'metaphysics of consciousness' commence only when the individual is 'thrown out, outside the being of the house, a circumstance in which the hostility of men and of the universe accumulates'.[75] But what Bachelard calls the 'cradle of the house' is for Edmond merely a narcotized existence while the liberated consciousness is quickly deformed. He accepts the image of release and self-definition, but his experience will not sustain it. Told by the fortune-teller that he is 'special', that he is not where he belongs, he sets out to fulfil a vague dream of selfhood, to escape a determinism into which he feels himself to be slipping. But his mentor is simply a man in a bar who offers the advice that the 'niggers have it easy' because they are outside the pressures of history and morality. He is a dubious guide to the underworld into which Edmond now plunges, though the various stages of the process towards liberation which he identifies (*Pussy ... Power ... Money ... adventure ... self-destruction ... religion ... release* ... ratification (p. 24)) are indeed enacted by Edmond, though in a purely ironic form. Far from finding release, indeed, he ends up in a prison cell, more securely trapped than he was at the beginning by simple routine. He does not 'get out'. Instead what freedom of action he imagines himself to have is taken from him.

In pursuit of experience Edmond visits a bar/brothel, a peepshow and a whorehouse. Everywhere he is cheated. Systematically abused, deceived and beaten, he finds no community of feeling, no compassion and no fulfilment. Pawning his ring, he buys a 'survival knife' with which he threatens a woman in the subway ('What am I? A dog? I'd like to slash your fucking *face*' (p. 58)). He then assaults a pimp who tries to rob him, pouring out a stream of racial abuse, and then kills a young woman who is as vulnerable as he is.

Edmond is a kind of ironic *Bildungsroman* in that its protagonist sets out on a quest for self-knowledge and experience which leaves him baffled and imprisoned. The rhetoric of existential liberation comes up against a reality which is crude and brutal. When the fortune-teller observes that 'the world seems to be crumbling around us' (p. 16), she introduces an element of cataclysm which grows throughout the play. The logic that transforms Edmond from a baffled, lonely and alienated individual into a killer is not simply that of a disaffected inadequate who breaks under the pressure of experience. Indeed, his ramblings in the prison cell are not without a certain perceptiveness. As he suggests,

> I think that all this *fear*, this fucking fear we feel must hide a wish... I think we are like birds. I think that humans are like birds. We suspect when there's going to be an *earthquake*. Birds know. They leave three days earlier. Something in their soul responds ... And I think, in our soul, *we, we* feel, we sense there is going to be ... a cataclysm. But we cannot flee. We're fearful. All the time. Because we can't trust what we know. That ringing. (*Pause.*) I think we feel. Something tells us. 'Get out of here.' (pp. 90–1)

The irony is that he becomes the thing he had once feared. He is a part of the cataclysm he had thought himself to be escaping, just as the characters in *American Buffalo* were evidence of the collapse of value they deplored: 'When we *fear* things I think that we *wish* for them. (*Pause.*) *Death*. Or "burglars"' (p. 89). Here, as in the earlier play, it is tempting to extend this logic into the world of geopolitics in which anxiety and fear are equally in danger of precipitating the feared apocalypse.

The characters in *Edmond* speak a curiously hybrid language. Part of the time they ramble semi-coherently, and part of the time they make remarks which go to the heart of Mamet's concerns. Since language has been so devalued, however, the problem, for the audience no less than for the characters, is to distinguish one from the other. The word 'pledge' refers not to a human commitment but to an item to be 'redeemed' from a pawnbroker; the word 'survival' relates to the knife with which he commits murder. Attempts to make contact are seen as a threat; games become fraudulent; love is denatured into commercial sex. He announces the necessity to '*live*' shortly before killing – indeed, violence becomes a means of convincing himself that he is truly alive.

Like Teach before him, Edmond laments that 'There is NO LAW . . . there is no *history* . . . there is just *now* . . . and if there is a *god* he may love the weak . . . but he respects the strong' (p. 71). Yet, of course, it is precisely the present – a world of sensation without consequences – that Edmond embraces, just as it is strength that he comes to admire, though he ends as the victim of his own violence. He becomes a spiritual booster, selling the need for awareness:

> You know how much of our life we're alive, you and me? *Nothing*. Two minutes out of the year . . . We've bred the lives out of ourselves. And we live in a fog. We live in a dream. Our life is a *school*house, and we're dead. (pp. 66–7)

This is a fair enough description of his own spiritual lassitude and the debased consciousness of those he encounters, but the conclusion he draws from the analysis is the superior freedom of the black race and the need to take violent action against a constraining fate. He feels the need to relieve himself of a responsibility to understand or to act according to rational principles, and thus he rejoices in the apocalypse that he prophesies: he revels in being relieved of an obligation to understand. When he is arrested, he is himself listening to a preacher – drawn to a faith that will lift the burden of responsibility from him.

Edmond acquires his knife as a protection from 'everyone'. His tensions and the terrible hermeticism of his experiences are expressed in the form rather than the content of his speeches. Trapped in a prison cell, he says, 'You know, you know, you know, you know we can't distinguish between *anxiety* and *fear*. Do you know what I mean? I don't mean fear. I mean, I *do* mean "fear", I don't mean *anxiety*' (p. 89). The circularities, the linguistic culs-de-sac, the stuttering incompletions reproduce his own sense of bafflement. He longs for a new world 'full of *life*. And *air*. Where people are *kind* to each other, and there's work to do. Where we grow up in *love*, and in security', but instead he kills the person who could offer him that hope. Asked why he does so, he is unable to answer, the disintegration of his sensibility being reflected in the collapse of language. The reiterated personal pronoun is a marker indicating the collapse of the very self that it seems to proclaim: 'I... (*Pause.*) I... (*Pause.*) I don't ... (*Pause.*) I ... (*Pause.*) I don't ... (*Pause.*) I don't ... (*Pause.*) I don't think ... (*Pause.*) I ... (*Pause.*)' (p. 97).

He is drawn towards violence as though it exerted some kind of irresistible pull, and, indeed, there is an exemplary force in that attraction, given the past and present record of American society. It is, after all, as Mamet has said, 'a very violent country full of a lot of hate. You can't put a Band-Aid on a suppurating wound. The morality of the theatre is to tell the truth as best you can. When you're not doing that, you're being immoral.'[76]

Mamet has said of this play:

> it is about life in New York City, which I don't like. It's a play about a guy trying to find some place he can be saved, a guy who's resigning because in every scene he casts off more and more of the veil of the world.[77]

It is hard to accept this description in its entirety. Edmond casts off the veil of the world only in the sense that he is systematically cheated and defrauded, but he seems to recognize that this is a natural extension of his own values, though he is blind to his own self-deceits. The play appears to end with Edmond reconciled to himself and with a new relationship (to a black prisoner), but this is scarcely salvation or safety, since he has been coerced into a relationship that makes him the 'wife' of his fellow inmate. He has simply reversed the roles of the first part of the play and is now more absolutely trapped in a smaller room than the one he had once sought to escape.

All the characters in the play are performers. As a bystander says of the street-corner card sharps: 'they're all part of an act' (p. 36). The B-girl, the peepshow performer, the pimp, the whore are all actors. The waitress killed by Edmond claims that she is in training as an actress, though this turns out to be an elaborate piece of self-deception, the theatre becoming in her mind a kind of therapy, a route to self-realization; she says: '*Because what you must ask respect for is yourself . . . For your feelings . . . And, and, and not be someone else*' (p. 71). Elsewhere, Mamet has said that 'The theatre . . . is in a very sorry state now because nobody wants to celebrate will.'[78] Plainly he sees a parallel between this failure of nerve at the level of art and a more profound social crisis. Certainly a theatre or a life based on respect for 'feelings' edges us towards the very totalitarianism which he fears to be the underside of anarchy.

In a way Edmond's is a debased version of the romantic quest, in the sense suggested by Byron: 'The great object of life is Sensation – to feel that we exist – even though in *pain*.' For Byron, 'it is this "craving void" which drives us to Gaming – to Battle – to Travel – to intemperate but keenly felt pursuits of every description whose principal attraction is the agitation inseparable from their accomplishment.'[79] But what has collapsed is the romantic synthesis. The self is no longer secure, nor is society taken to defer to the pure rebel who initiates change at the level of the imagination. The language of the self-sufficient individual survives; the reality does not. Society seems little more than an aggregation of isolated beings fighting for satisfaction and survival. As Saul Bellow's Mr Sammler observes, it is a civilization assaulted

> in the name of reason and in the name of irrationality, in the name of visceral depth, in the name of sex, in the name of perfect and instant freedom . . . limitless demand – insatiability, refusal of the doomed creature (death being sure and final) to go away from this world unsatisfied. A full bill of demand and complaint was therefore presented by each individual. Non-negotiable. Recognizing no scarcity in any other human department.[80]

This is essentially the world in which Edmond exists. He is not, like many of Bellow's characters, an intellectual, potentially betraying the values he should be asserting; he is a baffled member of the bourgeoisie awakened from boredom in order to plunge into corruption – not a cosmic victim nor yet a simple product of social neglect or economic deprivation, but a wilful product of his own self-obsession, pursuing a logic that seems to promise access to meaning.

Edmond is reminiscent of James Purdy's *Malcolm* as adapted for the stage by Edward Albee. That too had offered a picaresque account of the destruction of its central character, slowly exposed to the corruptions of American society. Dependent as it was on a series of grotesques for which Albee never found an adequate dramatic equivalent, it failed. In Mamet's play the grotesques are not the product of a gothic sensibility. They are rooted all too clearly in a sense of the real, deformed only by the pressure of a dramatic foreshortening. Episode builds on episode as an artist constructs a painting from individual gestures. The sound of the play is established from the dissonant voices of those who demand, cajole and plead. Desire and experience cannot be brought into alignment, and the evidence lies both in that dissonance and in the theatrical space the individual characters keep between them. Need should generate trust, but betrayal and fear of betrayal are bred into Mamet's characters. Edmond moves from domination to submission, but neither stance creates the harmony or establishes the connection that he needs but dare not claim.

His failure to relate his fragmented experiences to some central meaning is equally the failure of his culture. Just as the individual fractures into sexual, social and economic roles, becoming thereby a dissociated sensibility suspended in time and space, so too does the society that he/she inhabits without joining. Mamet writes of a world in which alienation is a fundamental experience; he creates plays in which that fact is reflected in the linguistic and theatrical structure. They are, indeed, episodic for more than structural reasons. Discontinuity, disjunction, a disruption of coherence at almost all levels is fundamental. Not the least of Mamet's achievements lies in the degree to which he has accommodated such convictions at the level of character, language, action and dramatic form.

Edmond was not a great success, except by contrast with another play produced in 1979, by far his most spectacular disaster to date – *Lone Canoe or The Explorer*. This received its première at the Goodman Theatre in Chicago when a drama critics' convention was in town. The derision with which the play was greeted left a scar not only on Mamet but also on its director, Greg Mosher. Based on a story by Jack London, it debates the moral responsibility of a nineteenth-century explorer who has chosen to desert his native country in order to live with a remote tribe. Savagery and civilization become ironic terms as the man is manipulated by an apparent emissary from his former life into destroying his own happiness and with it, possibly, the happiness of the tribe, which is, anyway, in a desperate plight.

The play offers little in the way of the linguistic subtlety and the originality of conception and character that had marked his earlier work. Although the story of a man who had achieved sudden and unexpected happiness only to have it snatched from him may have had a personal relevance to a man whose own success had been precipitate, what was missing from the play was precisely a sense of commitment which could animate it. In a way it is an old-fashioned play of the kind he has occasionally suggested that he would like to write. There is action – violent action. There is suspense, as key information is suppressed, only to be released at critical moments like a time-capsule drug. What is missing is any sense that the fate of these characters matters to anyone, least of all to Mamet himself. We are told rather than shown crucial aspects of their lives, while the language they speak slips too often and too easily into bathos. Mamet is an incredibly prolific writer. His agent's files, like those of the Goodman Theatre, are full of unproduced plays, fragments of dialogue, half-developed ideas. Perhaps it is inevitable that from time to time one of these will make their way into the theatre prematurely. *Lone Canoe* was one such. The shock was so severe that for a while he turned to film scripts. But when he returned to the theatre four years later it was with his most impressive play to date – *Glengarry, Glen Ross*.

7

'GLENGARRY, GLEN ROSS'

To me the play is about a society based on business . . . a society with only one bottom line: How much money you make.[81]

The purpose of the theater is not primarily to deal with social issues . . . it's to deal with spiritual issues. I don't write plays to dump on people. I write plays about people whom I love and am fascinated by.[82]

Speaking of *American Buffalo* and of his later Pulitzer-Prize-winning work, *Glengarry, Glen Ross*, Mamet has said that both plays are 'set deeply in the milieu of capitalism, obviously an idea whose time has come and gone'. As he explained,

> in America we're still suffering from loving a frontier ethic – that is to say, take the land from the Indians and give it to the railroad. Take the money from the blacks and give it to the rich. The ethic was always something for nothing. It never really existed when the American frontier was open . . . it never was anything more transcendent than something for nothing. . . . The idea of go West and make your fortune, there's gold lying in the ground, was an idea promulgated by the storekeepers in the gold rush and the railroads in the westward expansion as a way of enslaving the common man and woman . . . playing on their greed. As W. C. Fields said, you can't cheat an honest man. So, because we've been rather dishonest about our basic desire to get something for nothing in this country we've always been enslaved by the myth of the happy capitalist. Familiar American pieties are always linked to criminality. That's why they're familiar American pieties.[83]

As this statement implies, there is a strain of pessimism in

Mamet's work, though it does battle with an equally powerful pull towards redemption. For the most part, sentimentality is rigorously excluded, his work being controlled by a governing irony. None the less, speaking of his plays, he chooses to stress a will to action and a desire for human relationship for which he can find little space in the plays themselves. The version of the past that he offers is one that proposes a wrong historical turn at the very beginning of the American Republic and a model of human relations subverted by social fiats. Somehow he wants to assert the possibility of change; he struggles to identify the small gesture which may prove the beginning of a recovery. In *American Buffalo* it is the relationship between Don and Bobby. In *Glengarry, Glen Ross* it is the evident need for faith by characters ostensibly cheated and betrayed. It is a slender hope, but it is all that he is able or willing to validate, and even then he is offering a gesture for which he can find little social or psychological justification.

David Mamet wrote *Glengarry, Glen Ross* a decade after *American Buffalo*, but it is very close to it in spirit. Like the earlier play it has its roots in Mamet's own experience. In 1969 he worked for a year in what he has called 'a fly-by-night operation which sold tracts of undeveloped land in Arizona and Florida to gullible Chicagoans'.[84] Worse than that, 'I sold worthless land to elderly people who couldn't afford it.' He was for a while uncertain about the play, and sent a copy to Harold Pinter, whose own enthusiasm was shared by the National Theatre in London, where it was premièred in 1983. It won two awards in England before opening on Broadway, where it won the Pulitzer Prize in 1984.

Running throughout Mark Twain's satire of American political and commercial corruption, *The Gilded Age*, is the chimera of 'the Tennessee lands', a tract of territory that quickly loses any reality and becomes the focus of financial speculation and an image of uncontrolled greed. In *Martin Chuzzlewit* Charles Dickens creates a similar symbol for a particular brand of American cupidity and calls it Eden, a phoney real-estate venture whose name captures precisely that blend of puritan zeal and fallen man which characterizes the American dream of instant wealth. As the aptly named General Choke observes, carefully blending piety, natural philosophy and greed: 'here am I with grey hairs, sir, and a moral sense. Would I, with my principles, invest capital in this speculation if I didn't think it full of hopes and chances for my brother man?'[85] In Mamet's play the real-estate tracts in Florida serve much the same function. Glengarry and Glen Ross sound and are designed to sound romantic and reliable. For the purchasers they represent hope and possibility; for the salesmen, not merely a living to be secured by any means, but also a drama in which they can act out their own fantasies. Partly confidence tricksters and partly fabulators, they spin stories and invent plausible narratives with all the energy and conviction of a writer. There is something in this double role which has made the figure of the salesman a compelling character in plays such as *The Iceman Cometh*, *Death of a Salesman* and *The Dark at the Top of the Stairs*; even Stanley Kowalsky in *A Streetcar Named Desire* is a salesman. On the one hand he represents a whole commercial system, a pivotal figure in the processes of exchange; on the other, he is the creator of myth whose stories must be compelling if he is to survive. He is Scheherazade. So long as he keeps talking, his hopes are alive and, to a degree, so are those of his listeners. For this reason it would be a mistake to see *Glengarry, Glen Ross* as simply an attack on American business ethics, though it is certainly that. The fact is that the will to believe is regarded as powerful and even potentially redemptive, and the ability to create fictions, though corrupted and corrupting, is seen as containing the essence of a possible transcendence. That such an impulse is aborted, misdirected so as to become a simple agent of capitalism, is the source of his social satire; that it has the power to entrance is the origin of a certain fascination and even exultance.

In a sense the real-estate operation is offered as a model of capitalist enterprise. The company has organized a competition among its salesmen. The winner receives a Cadillac and the runner-up a set of steak knives. The losers are to be fired. The elegant simplicity of this arrangement serves to expose the operation of a system in which success, defined in purely financial terms, is rewarded, and failure summarily punished. Placed under this kind of intense pressure, one of the salesmen proposes a robbery that will secure the addresses of prospective customers, itself a key to success. The fact that the successful salesmen are given the best addresses also serves to underline a basic tenet of this society: to those that hath shall be given. But criminality is not merely a result of competition; it is an essential element of the business. Mamet explained of his own experience as someone whose job it was to judge the income and sales susceptibility of potential customers: 'This appointment was called a *lead* – in the same way that a clue in a criminal case is called a *lead* – i.e. it may lead to the suspect, the suspect in this case being a *prospect*.'[86] The confusion of realms is clearly deliberate, so that the actual crime involved in robbing the real-estate office is merely an objectification of the crimes daily perpetrated in the name of business.

Mamet's characters are forced to treat as real the fictions they promulgate. They live on their wits and are, indeed, brilliant performers. When a customer unexpectedly walks into the office in an attempt to reclaim his money, they move effortlessly into a routine, constructing an instant drama in which, like actors, they depend on one another, for brief moments laying aside their anxieties, although those anxieties may provide the motor force. The customer himself – James Lingk – though thoroughly deceived by the real-estate salesmen and harassed by his wife, has a will to believe, a need for faith, which is not wholly negated by his betrayal. Indeed, on some level that need is shared even by those who seek to deceive him. The problem is that they no longer have access to a vocabulary which can express that need; they are themselves the victims of a system in which they are turned against one another. Pressed back against the reality of their situation, they become desperate, self-obsessed, self-justifying. Released into their roles as storytellers, they become brilliantly inventive, creating personae much as a playwright creates characters.

The play is prefaced by what is described as a practical sales maxim – 'Always Be Closing'. The essence of salesmanship, in other words, is to imply both that the customer is getting a bargain and that he or she is in a position to take advantage of the seller. The relationship is one in which the customer is offered the illusion of power; it takes as its premiss the exploitative nature of human relationships. The play thus in part becomes concerned with those relationships and the systems of power which they expose.

Structurally, the first act is built around a series of encounters between pairs of characters – a familiar strategy for Mamet, who seems happiest when orchestrating two voices. What appears to fascinate him is the pattern of power that emerges in such relationships – the extent to which dominance and subservience are established independently of the lexical content of exchanges. The opening scene, which takes place in a Chinese restaurant, provides brilliant evidence for this. Shelly Levine, a salesman in his fifties, is facing the imminent possibility of dismissal. Like Willy Loman, he boasts of past success but, unlike Willy, he can see all too clearly the abyss that is opening up in front of him. He appeals for help to John Williamson, a man ten years younger than him and responsible for assigning potential customers to individual salesmen. For the first five or ten minutes Levine and Williamson converse in a virtually incomprehensible jargon, speaking of 'leads', 'the board', 'closing', 'sheets', 'cold calling', 'six and ten' and 'Glengarry', but for all this the power relationship emerges clearly enough, this being more important than the precise context of that relationship. Levine tries to shore up his disintegrating world with words, but the flow of language shatters on Williamson's laconic and almost monosyllabic replies. Increasingly desperate, Levine begins to abuse him. In the course of the scene he tries appeal, intimidation, camaraderie and finally bribery; this shifting strategy is reflected in the tone, the volume and the rhythm of the exchanges rather than their content. Baffled by the arcane technical references of the real-estate business, the audience is forced to respond at a wholly different level (rather as in the interrogation scene of Pinter's *The Birthday Party*), while the desire to break the code creates a pressure that sustains audience interest no less powerfully than does plot revelation. Levine asks to be judged independently of his achievements, but in the brutally existential world of the salesman this is a nonsense: he is not merely what he has done but more vitally what he is doing now. His language suggests a total confidence at odds with his situation. Words flow one way, sense the other. In a way, that is the basic position of the salesman. The customer – who has the purchasing power – is largely silent. The salesman has to construct an alternative world with nothing more substantial than words.

He is an actor entirely dependent on his audience for survival, and survival is very much a concern in *Glengarry, Glen Ross*.

Caught up in their daily rituals, the characters are never able to question the ultimate purpose of their activity. They are themselves primary evidence for the function they serve; that is, they endeavour to create artificial needs and then offer to satisfy them. Thus it is that Mamet, speaking of *American Buffalo* but with obvious relevance to *Glengarry, Glen Ross*, remarked:

> it's the same thing that goes on in board rooms all over this country. It's the same thing that goes on in advertising agencies. . . . How can we get the American people to bend over. If we win . . . we're successful and we give ourselves awards in advertising and we give ourselves awards in the motion picture academy. . . . And we give ourselves awards in [the form of] a weekend at Palm Beach. And if we lose, we're on the unemployment lines and we're having food stamps and poverty comes in the door and love goes out the window. But what's the difference? I mean what are we trying to succeed in aid of?[87]

But this question cannot be asked by the characters in *Glengarry, Glen Ross*, not just because it implies a level of self-doubt that would be destructive of their performances – which must carry total conviction – but because they don't have access to a language in which such a question could be formulated. The need is real and emerges briefly, but there seems to be no mechanism to translate it into action, no vocabulary beyond an apologetic word here and there, a lament over betrayals perpetrated. Perhaps the most significant moment in this regard comes when one of the characters refuses to name his accomplice – when, in other words, he refuses to speak and opts for silence. There is evidently an honesty in this silence which is not there in speech. Certainly, when other values appear to be acknowledged and invoked, as at times they are, and the whole commercial system challenged, it quickly becomes apparent that this is merely a ploy to coerce a colleague or deceive a customer. Philosophy, language and morality are prostituted. Yet Mamet's salesmen are conscious of some deficiency, and they do glimpse another world of possibility, albeit one distorted by materialism.

What drives them is not merely need but a curiously distorted utopianism. Moss, another of the threatened salesmen, also in his fifties, speaks of the single rich customer he has always been seeking, who will transform his life in ways he does not choose to define. Glen Ross itself had been their ideal real-estate project, as Glengarry appears to be in the present. But they have to live with the failure of utopia. Moss's rich man never materializes; Glen Ross was 'fucked . . . up', and they cannot get access to Glengarry, which is preserved for their more successful colleagues.

Values are subtly distorted. David Moss rails against those who want to 'rob everybody blind' because it is bad for business. Friendship is consolidated by shared prejudices and shades easily into conspiracy. Spiritual need and family relationships are acknowledged merely as a prelude to a sales pitch or to provide moral leverage. When Moss announces, as he does in an early version of the play, that 'the establishment keeps you enslaved',[88] this is a justification for robbery rather than a political observation.

In the second scene, which also takes place in the Chinese restaurant, Moss and George Aaronow, both threatened with dismissal, discuss their plight. Aaronow says little, merely echoing Moss's complaints and reinforcing his prejudices, but he gradually finds himself ensnared in Moss's plan to rob the company, much as he would himself try to ensnare a customer seeking a property. Moss creates a word picture whose logic is directed to securing Aaronow's compliance. Indeed language is so pliable that (at least in a pre-production typescript), like other Mamet characters, he manages to contradict himself within the same speech. Asked by an increasingly alarmed Aaronow whether the project robbery is a genuine plan, already discussed with and agreed by the owner of a competing company, or simply speculation (a distinction reduced to a discussion of whether they are 'actually *talking* about this' or 'just speaking about it' (p. 39), Moss replies:

> What am I going to *talk* to him about, what am I going to *sell* him, and why should I talk to him the *first* place, I was going

to steal the leads I'd, wouldn't you, keep them for *yourself*? And *if* I talked to him, so *what*, I'd go and steal the leads I didn't know that I couldn't sell them.[89]

In the published version the speech is shortened, fragmented, the staccato rhythm of the exchange preventing Aaronow from challenging him with the contradiction.

Denial becomes assertion, Aaronow being pulled into culpability through the vortex of language. And, having secured Aaronow's promise not to betray him, Moss calmly insists that he, on the contrary, will do so if Aaronow refuses to collaborate, that he is already an accessory by virtue of having listened to the proposal. Relationship, it seems, is a trap, communication a snare and friendship a means of facilitating betrayal. Certainly the next scene, the most brilliant in an accomplished play, seems to demonstrate this, as the audience, no less than the potential customer, is deceived and implicitly betrayed by Richard Roma, one of the thrusting young salesmen who, like the actual salesmen with whom Mamet had worked, could 'sell you cancer'.

Also set, like the first two scenes, in the Chinese restaurant, it consists of an encounter between Roma and James Lingk, each sitting in a separate booth. Since neither character has appeared before, the audience has to construct character and relationship from language alone. Physically the scene suggests the growth of mutuality between two separate and possibly lonely people. In the course of the scene they leave their separate tables. The conversation is dominated by Roma, whose rambling speech seems to constitute a kind of philosophic statement. An improbable amalgam of sentimentality and down-market existentialism, it none the less touches on areas of genuine anxiety. 'What is it that we're afraid of?' he asks, and answers, 'Loss?' A central question, he suggests, is 'How can I be secure?' Seeming to disavow a concern for material gain ('That's a sickness. That's a trap'), he propounds a simple belief: 'I say *this* is how we must act. I do those things which seem correct to me *today*. I trust myself. And if security concerns me, I do that which *today* I think will make me secure' (p. 49). He urges the necessity to act without fear, to respond to the variety of life as 'a carnival', and to accept that the mere variety of experience is a testament to the fact that 'we're all different'. Lingk, sitting alone at his table, plainly responds to this speech, not perhaps so much for its content as for its implied message of new-found relationship. But when Roma suddenly flourishes a map of Florida and goes into a sales pitch ('What is that? Florida . . . This is a piece of land' (pp. 50–1)) the betrayal extends to the audience, suddenly forced to re-evaluate as simple pieties what it had taken for genuine truths. That kind of human betrayal – that apparent denial of the function of language – is a central concern of the play.

Roma is close kin to Saul Bellow's charlatan Dr Tamkin in *Seize the Day*, as to Melville's Confidence Man or Ralph Ellison's Rinehart in *Invisible Man*. His deceits are practised through language, but they stand as evidence both of human greed and of a human need for reassurance, comfort and trust. The potency of Roma's approach derives from the accuracy of his analysis. There are indeed crucial absences in people's lives, as there are areas of acute anxiety. He recognizes that what he is selling is not real estate but hope and consolation. Like O'Neill's Hickey he presents himself as a huckster for truth, but where Hickey sought self-justification Roma seeks profit. What masquerades as intimacy is in fact the betrayal of intimacy, confidence, trust, the shared experience implied by language. Like the characters in *American Buffalo* who lamented the anarchy to which they contributed, the salesmen in *Glengarry, Glen Ross* angrily attack the inhumanity of a system whose principles they have long since internalized.

In the whole third scene James Lingk hardly speaks (he utters just thirteen words), and yet, as we later discover, he feels that some kind of relationship has been established, some kind of human contract implied. Browbeaten by his wife to renege on the deal which Roma eventually persuades them to sign, he arrives at the real-estate office in person, apologetic over the failure of trust which his action implies. But Levine, who had taught Roma his craft, employs the same tactics as his pupil, beginning his sales pitch by insisting that 'You have to believe in yourself' (p. 67). The property becomes a dream to be claimed: 'This is that *thing* that you've been dreaming of, you're going to find that suitcase on the train, the guy comes in the door, the bag that's full of money' (p. 72). Greed is transformed into an existential quest: his customers are told that they have 'met possi*bi*lity' and that 'Now is the time' (pp. 73–4). But the very moment they seize this hope they are betrayed: 'they wilted all at once . . . they both kind of *imperceptibly slumped*' (p. 74). This defeat is welcomed as marking Levine's return to the pack, his success turning on the defeat of his customers. The challenge of the sale is transposed into a mock-heroic language, as Levine accuses Williamson of lacking the courage and will demanded by the chase, an accusation that is more direct in the typescript than in the published version: 'You don't have the *blood*, John. You don't have the *blood* . . . You haven't been there and you can't *go* there. Never *been* out there . . . you don't know what it is . . . you don't have the balls.'[90]

The salesmen see themselves as existential heroes whose status and identity derive from what they do; mythic figures, they depend on their own resources and a simple world of male companionship which they describe in terms more suitable to a street cop: 'You have to learn it on the streets . . . 'Cause your partner *depends* on it . . . you can't exist alone' (pp. 97–8). Roma sees himself as the last of the frontiersmen in a world which has surrendered to mediocrity: 'it's not a world of men . . . it's a world of clock watchers, bureaucrats office holders. What it is, it's a fucked up world . . . there's no adventure *to* it . . . Dying breed' (p. 105). In a sense they are right. They are the inheritors of that ethos, but, like Arthur Miller's ageing cowboy in *The Misfits*, they use their talents for a squalid end. The protagonist of Miller's film captures wild horses for dog food; they stake their fortunes and possibly their lives (Levine seems to have considered suicide) on nothing more adventurous than selling land (valuable or worthless) to people who are themselves seduced by an old dream, an avaricious myth of sudden profit. If, as Fitzgerald hinted in *The Great Gatsby* and *Tender is the Night*, that dream was tainted in the beginning, there is, however, still a seductive dignity (not untouched by pathos) in those who can convince themselves as well as others that fantasy has its own authority. To be sure, in the end the consequence is almost wholly destructive, but there is none the less a fascination in witnessing those who can invent a world with nothing more substantial than words. It was the dubious fascination of Gatsby, who inhabited a world constructed by his own imagination; it is equally the fascination of Mamet's characters, which implicates the audience in just the same way as the reader is seduced into complicity with Gatsby. Imaginative intensity detached from morality retains a dangerous attraction, and just as Fitzgerald was aware of the significance of this for the writer so, too, was Mamet.

Nor does Mamet write about his salesmen with contempt. They invent to survive. It is what they do. And as a writer he is close enough to that world to acknowledge its pressure, to recognize the exhilaration that may derive from a fiction convincingly constructed, from a work whose rhythms compel attention and even belief. He too is in a sense a salesman, and something of Hickey's contradictions also exist in his world. The man who has said that, as a playwright, he wanted to 'be by myself and do my own thing and create my own plays and be with my friends. We lived on our wits' is likely to feel something in common with a group of salesmen who at base want very little else.

Mamet's salesmen are improvisational actors. When the robbery necessitates the renegotiation of contracts, they prepare to stage a masquerade in which one of the executives will 'be the *president*, just come *in* from out of *town*' (p. 62). When James Lingk arrives to revoke his contract, Roma and Levine improvise a drama in which Levine plays the role of an American Express executive – a satisfied and important customer – and Roma that of a friend of the rich and influential. His own actual experience with a real-estate company had indeed taught Mamet that 'the salesmen were primarily performers. They went into people's living rooms and performed their play about the investment properties.'[91] Though these dramas are designed to deceive and stem from the need to survive, inevitably this raises a question about the status of the play in which these scenes occur, for the salesman's performance, his fictions, his deceptions, are matched by those of the writer.

The English actor Jack Shepard, who played the part of Richard Roma in the British première, commented, interestingly, of the play that 'The rhythms are slick, fast, syncopated, like a drum solo... What's missing is the tune.'[92] This is precisely the tone of a play in which, moment by moment, each character has a clear objective – the almost sexual seduction of the buyer by the salesman, the need to succeed in the sales competition, and so on – but in which no character has any real sense of purpose. In the name of what (beyond simple survival) is this activity undertaken? What lies beyond the closing of the deal? Indeed, closure becomes a central image. Each moment is sealed off from the next. Each completed deal merely precipitates another. They serve nothing but the system established by the absent owners who set the mechanism in motion but who, like Godot, never appear. There is indeed no tune, and much the same could have been said of *Sexual Perversity in Chicago* and *American Buffalo*. To set against this we have only two gestures – that of James Lingk, regretting the betrayal of what he imagines to be a genuine friendship, and that of George Aaronow, who knows precisely who committed or conspired in the crime but who refuses to name him out of loyalty, a commitment which is plainly misplaced but which stems from real feeling. When John Lahr suggests that Teach's summary of human potential ('We're just savage shit-heads in the wilderness') is an accurate account, he forgets such fragile moments of possibility.

Mamet has said of *Glengarry, Glen Ross* that

> It has been suggested to me that the play concerns American cut-throat capitalism, and that its theme is the destructiveness of competition. I suppose this is a logical interpretation and is probably true into the bargain. All that I set out to do was write about my experiences in a real estate office, and I assure you that as bizarre as the behaviour in the play might seem the behaviour in the office itself made it look tame.[93]

The remarks are calculatedly disingenuous. Though it is based on his own experiences and certainly offers a caustic view of American capitalism, the play's concerns go further than this. Behind the fast-paced patter of the salesmen is a desperation which is not simply the product of a competitive society. His salesmen are agents of the capitalist system which is destroying them; but they are also brilliant storytellers, improvising their lives, performing themselves and deploying language with a facility matched only by its misplaced function. The status of the salesmen is determined solely by their success, but it is in failure that anxieties are exposed, as the flow of language falters. They are not only selling property to other people but also struggling to maintain a sense of identity and meaning independent of that activity.

The problem is that they have so thoroughly plundered the language of private need and self-fulfilment and deployed it for the purpose of deceit and betrayal that they no longer have access to words that will articulate their feelings. (When Roma tries to prevent Lingk from bowing to his wife's demands, he applies the language of commerce to private relationships: 'Your life is your own. You have a contract with your wife. You have certain things you do *jointly*, you have a bond there . . . and there are *other* things. Those things are yours (p. 93).) They have bent language back against the joint and it no longer serves its purpose to communicate genuine need. Roma regards as 'admirable' Levine's spontaneous lies and his skill in using deceit to achieve a sale. Failure is defined as an inability to convince people of their need to purchase land of dubious value; success as the reverse. To steal the company's files is a criminal offence; to deceive clients is simply good business. There is no moral law, only a system of reward and punishment. In the name of a social function, an idea or an organization they are willing to betray an essential humanity. Thus Mamet has said that

> The code of an institution ratifies us in acting amorally, as any guilt which might arise out of our acts would be borne not by ourselves but shared out through the institution. We have it somehow in our nature, Tolstoy wrote, to perform horrendous acts which he would never dream of as individuals, and thus if they are done in the name of some larger group, a *state*, a *company*, a team, that those vile acts are somehow magically transformed and become praiseworthy.[94]

Whatever bafflement Mamet may have caused, reviewers and critics are all agreed on his sensitivity to language. Dialogue is reproduced in all its inarticulateness. Characters speak in sentence fragments, contradict themselves and abandon thoughts in midstream. They reach for a vocabulary that they can barely command. The most common punctuation mark in the printed text is the comma, as mismatched phrases and random ideas are strung together in a protective flow of sound. Mamet's characters tend to stutter and to address themselves almost as much as others. At first sight a page of his text looks remarkably like a transcription of actual speech, and this had led to the presumption that he is in essence a naturalistic writer, faithfully reproducing the tones and speech patterns of urban America. But he is never simply this. The language is carefully shaped – 'a line's got to scan. I'm very concerned with the metric scansion of everything I write, including the rhythmic emphasis of the word "fucking". In rehearsal I've been known to be caught counting the beats on my fingers.'[95] Increasingly he has felt able to pare down that speech, to eliminate words and leave ever greater spaces ('the whole truth lies in what you leave out'). In part this does serve the interest of psychological realism. Thus when an ageing salesman feels control slipping away from him his language begins to disintegrate: 'I'm, I'm, I'm, I'm fucked on the board. *You.* You see how . . . I . . . (*Pause.*) I can't . . . my mind must be in other places. 'Cause I can't do any . . . I can't close 'em' (p. 56). But, paradoxically, the collapse of language exposes a truth concealed by words. As in Albee's *Who's Afraid of Virginia Woolf?* contact only seems possible when the deceits of language are laid aside. Although Mamet has said of their aphasic language as of their scatological dialogue that 'The people who speak that way tell the truth' because 'They don't institutionalize thought. They speak from a sense of need',[96] that need, together with his characters' failure to satisfy it or even see with any clarity how it might be satisfied, provides his principal subject, while language and deceit are presented in some fundamental way as coeval.

Discussing the structure of Chekhov's work, Robert Corrigan spoke of contextual or concentric action; his characters live lives of radical discontinuity and incomplete experience, and his plays focus on situation rather than plot, a condition of being rather than a process. Something similar might be said of Mamet's work. Things plainly happen but, in terms of a sequence of events, not a great deal. In *Duck Variations, Dark Pony, Reunion, A Life in the Theatre* and *American Buffalo,* indeed in most of his plays, physical action is minimized, linear development relatively insignificant, and ironic endings tend to bend the action towards circularity. In *Duck Variations* and *American Buffalo* the characters end much as they begin. In *A Life in the Theatre* the characters have changed places but otherwise things remain much the same. In *Glengarry, Glen Ross*, despite the fact that the planned robbery is carried out, nothing has altered. The same values apply; no one is released from the governing irony. The play thus ends not with the unveiling of the criminal but with Roma's casual remark that he is going to the Chinese restaurant, where, of course, the play began. Such a circularity clearly reflects the production–consumption cycle of capitalism; it also suggests a more profound and disturbing hermeticism, and that hermeticism – as presumption and fact – underlies so much of Mamet's work, and defines the context in which his characters live their lives.

For Mamet himself the achievement of *Glengarry, Glen Ross* lies in his ability to construct a play which, at least in its second act, creates a form that would have pleased a Terence Rattigan or a Sidney Kingsley. 'People love my new play', he has said, 'because I finally had the will to write a second act. I wrote a million episodic plays. I can write them with my left hand. So what? Who cares? Fortunately, I got sick of it before [the audience] did.'[97] It was the admixture of an episodic first act and a conventionally structured second which had first caused him to doubt its dramatic viability. Despite the accomplishment of this play, however, it is difficult to understand his anxiety to work within conventional forms. It is true that those he most admires in the theatre have chosen to do precisely that, using those very conventions while subverting the assumptions they raise. But so much of Mamet's originality lies in what he takes to be his faults that it is hard to share his enthusiasm for what he sees as the craftsmanship associated with maintaining the dramatic unities. Part of the effect of *Glengarry, Glen Ross* itself comes from an opening act in which the separate scenes create a series of overlapping and interrelating versions of the real. There is, to be sure, an element of the thriller about the play. Those who had regretted the absence of narrative drive were rewarded by a drama in which the planning and unravelling of a crime provide some of the energy and compulsion of the work. But the real fascination remained the individual moments, the tainted arias, the brilliantly corrupt performances of characters who have invested their lives rather than their money in the dreams they present to others. And that did not in essence depend upon conventionality of structure.

8

CONCLUSIONS

Mamet's characters are never wholly definable; they are composed of contrary impulses. They may use language to deny the purpose of language, but the necessity for faith, for trust, for simple human contact on which they depend to practise their deceits, is a need they also feel themselves. They are confidence tricksters, but confidence is something that they too desire. Each emotion contains its contrary, each act its denial. And so his characters enter into marriage in search of a love whose demands they must resist. They betray a trust on which they depend for their comfort. Yet that act of betrayal never wholly destroys the faith they manipulate, the innocence they affect to despise, the need they seem to deny. Very often the necessity for companionship or faith is put into the mouths of those most destructive of such values (Teach in *American Buffalo*; Roma in *Glengarry, Glen Ross*), those most dedicated to abrogating them. Their cynicism is, however, an acknowledgement of the potency of such values. The confidence trickster may deny a fundamental human contract, but he can do so only at the price of recognizing its existence and, ultimately, its resilience. If this has proved true of a number of his works, then it was especially so of a play that he completed in 1985, a play in which the need for a restored intimacy ultimately triumphs over the impulse to exploit it. *The Shawl*, completed and first performed in 1985, is a subtle and ultimately a lyrical work in which faith is both betrayed and vindicated.

Once again we have a literal confidence trickster, or so it appears. John claims clairvoyant powers, though, in fact, this is apparently just a device for restoring his fortunes and consolidating what is apparently a homosexual affair. In his fifties and evidently clinging on to the tenuous affections of a man twenty years younger, he needs to offer some inducement for the relationship he plainly needs. This, it seems, is the cash he can win from his clients. He is consulted by Miss A, whose own motives are mixed. She wishes to get in touch with her dead mother, in part because she wants to seek confirmation of her desire to challenge her mother's will, but also because she wants an explanation for the failure of love implicit in the lost inheritance. Slowly he secures her confidence, building a picture of her life from small clues and, where that is insufficient, from research. Her need to believe is so great that it even survives her catching him in an error. She needs someone she can trust. As does John.

But Mamet, too, is a trickster. The emotions his play provokes, the imaginations he stirs, are the product of calculation and professional skill. Indeed, when John explains his methods to his companion, Charles, there is, perhaps, some relevance to the playwright's situation. 'How *legitimate* is that thing which I do?' he asks.

> I *show* you the trick 'from the back', and you're disappointed. Of course you are. If you view it as a 'member of the audience'. One of the, you will see, the most painful sides of, the profession is this: you do your work well, and who will see it? No one, really . . . what separates us, finally, is we look *clearly*. So be it. Not that we're 'special'. (p. 22)

That could stand not only as Mamet's justification of his own profession but also as his explanation of how trust and betrayal can coexist; beyond that it stands as a Whitmanesque reminder that, as John remarks of Miss A, we too 'can see. Those very things which are before our eyes.' From the deceits of art are born truths.

However, there do remain mysteries, since art no less than experience reveals itself as more than the sum of its parts. So, here, the trickster becomes more than that. At the end he seems to reveal a genuine clairvoyance, a hint of the poetry that lies behind the calculation. The play ends with the two of them together still exploring the narrative of her life. Charles, it seems, has gone. All that is left is a man and a woman pulled together by needs which are not entirely mutual but which are satisfied in some degree by a relationship that offers something more than consolation. What they jointly seek is some kind of absolution; the wonder is that, for all the guilts, the betrayals and deceits, they seem on the very brink of offering it to one another.

Structurally, the play could scarcely be more simple. We learn little of the past history of any of the characters. The figure of Charles comes close to being merely a dramatic convenience. Strictly speaking there is only the minimum of 'action', and yet *The Shawl* is compelling. At first it seems like an artist's sketch for a painting, which will later add detail, colour, depth. But there is a clarity of line and a grace of execution that make further development redundant. The sense of mystery may generate and sustain our attention; the refusal to resolve it is crucial. The furious pace of so many of his plays is here stilled. The result is a work of genuine lyricism, a tone poem which shows, if that were needed, that Mamet's skills with language extend beyond the stuttering incompletions of urban America, and which underlines the extent to which the need for faith is a motivating force and primary objective of characters whose lives may otherwise suggest the collapse of all values and the eclipse of all hope.

*

David Mamet likes to see himself as responsive to the pressures that have deformed national purpose no less than private needs. He is concerned with the texture of experience, as he is with locating his characters in a familiar linguistic and social environment. But, just as he is more concerned with the extent to which that environment is a product rather than the cause of a fundamental failure of will, so he is not best viewed as proposing radical solutions to evils seen as purely a consequence of capitalism, the result of a wrong historical turn. The self-deceits practised by his characters, their manifest vulnerability, their aggressions, directed at others but destabilizing their own security, are rooted in something more profound than forms of economic organization. To be sure, they are exacerbated by a system which seemingly subordinates the spiritual to the material, but the spaces that have plainly opened up in their lives are a product of more than social and economic alienation. Like Willy Loman in *Death of a Salesman*, they have all the wrong dreams, but the need to dream, the psychological and spiritual emptiness that invites a material solution, is rooted in more disturbing experience. Mamet's characters are partly the victims of social process, but other pressures threaten to deform their sensibilities and intimidate them into conspiring in their own irrelevance. Above all, they are frightened of death and its power retrospectively to drain all experience of meaning. Accordingly they are committed to the endless task of seeking justification for their own existence.

Freud once proposed the possibility of psychoanalysing an entire society suffering from what he called a 'social neurosis', asking:

> If the evolution of civilization ... has such a far-reaching similarity with the development of an individual, and if the same methods are employed in both, would not the diagnosis be justified that many systems of civilization or epochs of it — possibly even the whole of humanity — have become 'neurotic' under the pressure of civilizing trends?[98]

In just such a sense, Mamet sets out to suggest that American society, in Freudian terms, has failed to progress from the adolescent to the adult level. Again, though, he is not content with such a proposition if it fails to acknowledge tensions and ironies which are not solely the product of 'civilizing trends', or fails to reveal a particular society caught in a regressive spiral. He speaks cogently and passionately of the morally and psychologically damaging pressures of American society, but he does not, like Arthur Miller, call for a moralized capitalism, or, like Tennessee Williams, for an amnesty for the pure in heart, a space in which the pragmatics of the public world may be momentarily suspended; nor does he look for structural change. Indeed, the irony is that the confident tone of his public pronouncements rarely invades his plays, which are painfully effective precisely because of the precision with which he reproduces the dislocations, the vacuity, the desperate strategies of those who are aware of some insufficiency in their lives but seemingly have access to no language with which they may fully express it, no actions which can assuage it, no sense of transcendence which may serve to neutralize it. And that failure of nerve, of language, of apprehension, of imagination is, to Mamet, as true and as fundamentally destabilizing on a private as on a public level, where the collapse of communality may edge the entire culture towards apocalypse.

Mamet's world is a denatured culture. It has an urban brittleness, a hysteria barely contained. It is a society in which the language of community survives, but not its reality. Friendship is invoked in name but denied in fact; teamwork is proposed as a model but contradicted in action. Sexual roles have been problematized. Sexual contact is apotheosized but feared. The social contracts of civilized life are appealed to but betrayed. Mamet's is, to a surprising degree, a male world. In some of his most powerful and original works there are no female characters. He may deplore the sexism of the American language no less than of American social behaviour but he frequently chooses to explore situations in which women find little or no place. That is in part, perhaps, a reflection of his own predilection for specifically male environments. Indeed his own epic poker nights suggest more than a hint of Stanley Kowalski. But, more crucially, it suggests the extent to which he sees his characters as being in thrall to destructive myths, adolescent and ultimately self-annihilating. Mamet's characters are rootless people; they lack a common past and a common present. Language fails them as they fail language; they can understand neither themselves nor those with whom they believe themselves to share a common view of experience. They are lonely, consoled only by the fictions they choose to regard as reality. They inhabit a recognizably modern world in which there is a disjunction between social rhythms and private needs. What was once, it is implied, an assumed community of interests and of being is now severely eroded. The only sustaining tension is provided by a delicate balancing act of mutual self-interest. The result is an alienation which strikes deeper than social anxieties, invading even the realm of the self at its most vulnerable. Sexuality is presented not as an expression of love but as a substitute for it; personal meaning is to be derived from the acquisition of goods at the minimum price (theft being the ultimate expression of this), and mutual reliance gives way to competition in which relationships are seen essentially in terms of commodity exchange, a negotiation in which maximum satisfaction is demanded for minimum outlay. Something has been lost, and that absence becomes the essence of Mamet's concern. Loss has to do with a defeat of the imagination, the moral being and the will. His characters seemingly lack all three. They are, for the most part, baffled and defeated; but seldom wholly so. There remains an impulse to resist, to invent a world whose necessities are other than those of the society in which they find themselves. And that impulse is crucial. It is what makes it possible for Mamet to represent himself as a social playwright, and to insist not merely upon the necessity but also the credibility of transformation – a transformation of which the theatre itself is in some respects a model. Though his plays detail the collapse of communality, their very processes demonstrate its possibility.

As he has said:

> In a morally bankrupt time we can help to change the habit of coercive and frightened action and substitute for it the habit of trust, self-reliance, and co-operation. If we are true to our ideals we can help to form an ideal society – a society based on and adhering to ethical first principles – not by *preaching* about it, but by *creating* it each night in front of the audience – by showing how it works. In action.[99]

The theatre becomes a moral lesson:

> the theatre is a profession of communion in the truth. That's why people come to the theatre. . . . You cultivate the habit of mutuality, of sharing things, of creating things – whether it is creating a scene or creating a theatre company with your partners. You're building a true theatre and becoming a mature man or woman.[100]

The question is whether this mutuality can survive the conditions of modern life, whether the myths of theatre can expose and counteract the illusions deployed by society, or whether, like so many examples of 1960s communitarian theatre, the communality of the theatre might prove not only factitious but also coercive, assaulting social myths in the name of systems of thought and behaviour scarcely less destructive than those they claim to oppose.

Perhaps he seeks to place rather too great a weight on the theatre. Certainly, his own presentation of the moral and spiritual failures of society is so powerful as to leave little room for the possibility of redemption, which he also wishes to assert. His analysis of people as semantic beings seems to imply that we are the victims of language; his dramatization of people as social beings stresses the degree to which we are the products of a fate which we seemingly invent in order to experience the will-less pleasure of submission. But resistance is plainly a central necessity to a writer who in effect accuses his fellow human beings of collaborating in their own irrelevance. Thus the primary function of the theatre, of acting and of being in the world, is to acknowledge a freedom which must first be recognized before it can become embraced for what it is:

> As the stoics say, generosity, correctness, accomplishment, mutuality, self-acceptance – you wish to become the excellent man or woman – what prevents you? Nothing. That's the one commandment of stoical philosophy which is the philosophy of acting. What prevents you? Nothing. Why tomorrow rather than today? What prevents you? Nothing.[101]

Asked what he would wish to leave with his audiences, he has said, 'I hope what I'm arguing for, finally and lately, has been an *a priori* spirituality. Let's look at the things that finally matter. We need to be loved; we need to be secure; we need to help each other; we need to work.' If there is no space in his plays where that spirituality can take concrete form – social form, in terms of how society is organized, or personal form, in that the individuals are left with the vacancies still present in their lives – Mamet's response is to say:

> Well, that's the problem.... Looking at the America in which I live and which you have to be left with at the end of the play ... [but] I would hope [I am offering] courage to look at the world around you and say I don't know what the hell the answer is but I'm willing to try to reduce all of my perspectives of the world around me to the proper place. After everything is said and done, we're human beings, and if we really want to we can find a way to get on with each other, to have the great, almost immeasurable, courage it takes ...

> to be honest about . . . our desires and not to institutionalize or abstract our relationships with each other.[102]

That this remains a tenuous hope is a measure of the bleakness of the world which he dramatizes; that he continues to assert it with such conviction is a testament to his belief that the theatre has a central role to play in social, moral and metaphysical terms. The logic of our experience may point to apocalypse; the fact of a counterveiling human necessity suggests the possibility of defeating that logic.

It is true that while he speaks of spirituality the immediate expression of that spirituality seems to lie in the restoration of human values and a reconstructed moral system. But that, of course, has conventionally been seen as both the route to, and evidence of, a grace which becomes the justification of existence. Christian ethics, Tolstoyan morality and libertarian convictions blend. Thus, while observing that 'Maybe what I'm saying in the plays is that human nature does not change, but individual nature does' he chooses to describe this process as 'redemption'. Its public expression may lie in a resistance to social coercions but its consequence is not only to clear the ground for personal relationships, in a world restructured to be responsive to human need, but also to resist the collapse of meaning at all levels. The fear which his characters so often feel is something more than losing whatever personal or public roles they may enjoy; it is a fear of having no meaning beyond those roles. That is the sense of alarm which informs *A Life in the Theatre* and *Edmond* no less than *Duck Variations* and *The Woods*. He is not concerned with a codified religious response to experience; what does seem to fascinate him is the need which his characters evidently feel for a sense of completion and coherence which not even relationships can fully satisfy. Finally the missing dimension which they feel rather than understand has to do with the fact that like Robert and John in *A Life in the Theatre* they perform in a world whose audience evidently left some time ago, abandoning them to themselves so that they must locate their meaning in being rather than performing, even if performance may provide a route back to that self.

For Mamet, theatre is not concerned with rational analysis. Its power, its technique and its special achievement lies in its ability to tackle issues felt on the pulse. As he has observed, 'Only if the question posed is one whose complexity and depth renders it unsusceptible to rational examination does the dramatic treatment seem to us appropriate, and the dramatic solution become enlightening.'[103] Just as the dream may be a response to unresolved psychological problems, so drama performs the same function on a social level. It engages the myths, the contradictions and the anxieties of society. It is not so much that it is a force for social change or an agent of political transformation as that it is a mechanism for perceiving truths which are lived but not always expressed or even perceived for what they are. In a period in which such anxieties are repressed, sublimated, displaced or chemically neutralized, the theatre potentially plays a crucial role.

Drama, he has said,

> is not an attempt to depict something which is real in the external world but rather an attempt to depict something which is real in an internal world. It's an attempt to deal symbolically with feelings, with thoughts about the world. . . . It's the difference between being a painter and an illustrator.[104]

It is in that sense that the most accomplished of his early plays, *American Buffalo*, could be considered a realist work. And, despite the dense clutter of objects which dominate the stage, in a way that recalls Arthur Miller's *The Price* or the realist productions of David Belasco, this, too, is not so much an attempt to recuperate the presumptions behind an exhausted style as an ironic commentary on those presumptions. It is also worth recalling Meyerhold's observation that 'The object does not exclude the symbol, on the contrary, as reality becomes more profound, it transcends its own reality. In other words, reality, in becoming supra-natural, is transformed into a symbol.'[105]

The musician John Cage used to wire chairs for sound and then amplify the resultant noises when people sat on them. The sounds were accurately reproduced but distorted through amplification. The very stress on the detailed reality of the sounds made them seem unreal. That perhaps is the sense in which Mamet is a realist. The very attention he draws to the language of his characters renders it strange, just as the detailed realism of a number of his stage sets draws attention to their factitiousness. Alain Robbe-Grillet has made much the same point about photography. Thus the familiar realism of the set in *American Buffalo* serves less to imply that character is a product of environment than to suggest the extent to which the characters are simple extensions of an object world. It underlines the absence of a human density to counterpose to that of the objects with which the stage is scattered. As they recycle language, repeat distorted and fragmentary banalities picked up from the media, his characters expose their own emptiness, their unreality. They become, in effect, no more than characters in a national drama, in a public myth. But, as Philip Roth once said, if 'it was fiction got us into this it was up to fiction to get us out of it again'. And so theatre is invoked to perform its allopathic function by creating on stage the communality that has been evacuated from the social world and demonstrating the fact of possibility in the very inventions of the imagination.

Mamet's accomplishment lies, at least in part, in the degree to which theatre becomes not merely the occasion of his art but also his subject. Acutely sensitive to the social pressures that shape the imagination, alert to the degree to which language deforms experience as experience determines language, he has created a series of plays which have addressed the nature of a modern experience that leaves the individual severed equally from the past and from the consolations of a shared present. Ironically, his plays themselves offer the moments of consonance whose absence is their central concern; even while exposing social and spiritual betrayals, he identifies a surviving will towards harmony, the shadow of a vision now only imperfectly perceived. Something has been lost, something vital. Between his characters and a clear understanding of what that might be lie an obscuring tangle of public myths, fantasies and deceits, a language drained of meaning, and a fear which blots out all sense of meaning and purpose. The process of his plays is one which identifies this obstruction to meaning and hope and which in its assumption of the minimum community constituted by the storyteller and the listener begins the urgent business of reconstruction.

NOTES

1 David Mamet in an interview with the author, December 1983.
2 Henry Hewes, National Theatre Study Notes for *Glengarry, Glen Ross* (1983), p. 2.
3 John Simon, ibid., p. 3.
4 David Mamet, *Current Biography* (August 1978), p. 27.
5 Interview with the author.
6 Quoted in Alfred Kazin, *An American Procession: The Major American Writers from 1830 to 1930 – The Crucial Century* (New York, 1985), p. 70.
7 Ibid., p. 120.
8 Ibid., p. 237.
9 David Mamet, Programme Notes, *Glengarry, Glen Ross* (1983).
10 *Dictionary of Literary Biography*, vol. 7 (1981), p. 65.
11 David Mamet, *New York Times*, 13 February 1977.
12 Robert Corrigan, *Introduction to Six Plays* (New York, 1979), p. xiv.
13 Interview with the author.
14 Samuel Beckett, *Proust: Three Dialogues* (London, 1965), p. 22.
15 Ibid., p. 28.
16 Ibid., p. 25.
17 Samuel Beckett, *I Can't Go On, I'll Go On*, ed. Richard W. Seaver (New York, 1976), p. 568.
18 Mel Gussow, *New York Times*, 19 October 1979.
19 David Mamet, *New York Times*, 15 January 1978.
20 David Mamet, *The Disappearance of the Jews* (c. 1982), typescript, p. 35.
21 Tom Wolfe, *Mid-Atlantic Man* (London, 1969), p. 88.
22 David Mamet, *New York Times*, 5 July 1976.
23 Ibid.
24 Quoted in Erich Fromm, *Beyond the Chains of Illusion:*

     My Encounter with Marx and Freud (New York, 1962), pp. 46–7.
25   Ibid., p. 51.
26   David Mamet, *New York Times*, 13 February 1977.
27   Interview with the author.
28   Richard Eder, *New York Times*, 12 March 1978.
29   Ibid.
30   Anton Chekhov, *Six Plays of Chekhov*, ed. Robert Corrigan (New York, 1979), p. 131.
31   *New York Times*, 17 March 1978.
32   David Mamet, *All Men Are Whores*, in *Short Plays and Monologues* (New York, 1981), pp. 71, 83.
33   David Mamet, Lecture (1979), typescript.
34   Daniel Bell, *The Cultural Contradictions of Capitalism* (London, 1976), p. 149.
35   *Dictionary of Literary Biography*, vol. 7 (1981), p. 66.
36   Ibid., p. 69.
37   David Mamet, *New York Times*, 6 July 1976.
38   David Mamet, *New York Times*, 15 January 1978.
39   Ibid.
40   David Mamet, 'Realism', typescript (n.d.).
41   Ibid.
42   David Mamet, *New York Times*, 15 January 1978.
43   Ibid.
44   Thorstein Veblen, *Theory of the Leisure Class: An Economic Study of Institutions* (London, 1925), p. 17.
45   Ibid., p. 28.
46   Joseph Bananno, *A Man of Honor: The Autobiography of a Godfather* (London, 1983), p. 63.
47   Ibid., p. 290.
48   National Theatre Study Notes, p. 4.
49   Alfred Sohn-Rethel, *Intellectual and Manual Labour: A Critique of Epistemology* (London, 1978), p. 41.
50   Oswald Spengler, *The Decline of the West*, trans. Charles Francis Atkinson (London, 1934), pp. 431, 463.
51   Ibid., p. 485.
52   Brendan Gill, 'No News from Lake Michigan', *The New Yorker*, 28 February 1977, p. 54.
53   Gordon Rogoff, 'Theatre – Albee and Mamet: The War of the Words', *The Saturday Review*, 2 April 1977.
54   David Mamet, *New York Times*, 15 January 1978.
55   Interview with the author.
56   Ibid.
57   Ibid.

58 David Mamet, note to *The Water Engine and Mr Happiness* (New York, 1978).
59 Interview with the author.
60 National Theatre Study Notes.
61 David Mamet, 'Concerning *A Life in the Theatre*', typescript, p. 4.
62 Ibid., p. 5.
63 David Mamet, *New York Times*, 16 October 1977.
64 David Mamet, *A Life in the Theatre* (New York, 1978).
65 David Mamet, Lecture 6, typescript, p. 5.
66 Christopher Lasch, *The Culture of Narcissism* (New York, 1979), p. xv.
67 Ibid., p. xvi.
68 Ibid.
69 Ibid.
70 Ibid., p. 9.
71 Ibid., p. 11.
72 Ibid., p. 14.
73 Ibid., p. 15.
74 Interview with the author.
75 Gaston Bachelard, *The Poetics of Space*, trans. Maria Jolas (Boston, Mass., 1969), p. 7.
76 Benedict Nightingale, 'Is Mamet the Bard of Modern Immorality?', *New York Times*, 1 April 1984.
77 Quoted in Daniel Bell, *The Cultural Contradictions of Capitalism* (London, 1976), p. 50.
78 David Mamet, Lecture 6, typescript, p. 4.
79 Quoted in Bell, op. cit., p. 17.
80 Quoted in ibid., p. 50.
81 David Mamet, *New York Times*, 28 March 1984.
82 David Mamet, *Ozark Magazine* (May 1984), p. 38.
83 Interview with the author.
84 National Theatre Study Notes, p. 7.
85 Charles Dickens, *Martin Chuzzlewit* (London, n.d.), pp. 299–300.
86 Programme Note, National Theatre (1983).
87 National Theatre Study Notes, p. 4.
88 *Glengarry, Glen Ross*, typescript, p. 31.
89 Ibid., pp. 38–9.
90 Ibid., p. 83.
91 National Theatre Study Notes, p. 7.
92 Ibid., p. 8.
93 Ibid., p. 7.
94 Interview with the author.

95 Ibid.
96 Programme Note, National Theatre (1983).
97 Jennifer Allen, 'David Mamet's Hard Sell', *New York*, 9 April 1984, p. 41.
98 Quoted in Erich Fromm, *Beyond the Chains of Illusion* (New York, 1962), p. 60.
99 David Mamet, 'First Principles', typescript, p. 5.
100 David Mamet, Lecture 6, typescript, p. 11.
101 Ibid.
102 Interview with the author.
103 David Mamet, 'A National Dream Life', *Dramatist Guild Quarterly*, 15 (Autumn 1978), p. 30.
104 Interview with the author.
105 Edward Braun, *The Theatre of Meyerhold: Revolution on the Modern Stage* (London, 1979), p. 98.

BIBLIOGRAPHY

WORKS BY DAVID MAMET

Plays

American Buffalo, Sexual Perversity in Chicago and Duck Variations. London: Methuen, 1978. *American Buffalo.* New York: Grove Press, 1977. *Sexual Perversity in Chicago* and *Duck Variations.* New York: Grove Press, 1978.
A Life in the Theatre. New York: Grove Press, 1978.
The Revenge of the Space Pandas and Binky Rudich and the Two-Speed Clock. Chicago: Dramatic Publishing Company, 1978.
The Water Engine and Mr Happiness. New York: Grove Press, 1978.
Reunion and Dark Pony. New York: Grove Press, 1979.
The Woods. New York: Grove Press, 1979.
Lone Canoe or The Explorer. Unpublished, 1979.
Lakeboat. New York: Grove Press, 1981.
The Poet and the Rent. New York: Samuel French, 1981.
Short Plays and Monologues (includes *Prairie Du Chien* and *All Men are Whores*). New York: Dramatists' Play Services, 1981.
Squirrels. New York: Samuel French, 1982.
The Disappearance of the Jews. Unpublished, 1982.
Edmond. New York: Grove Press, 1983.
The Frog Prince. New York: Samuel French, 1983.
The Spanish Prisoner. Unpublished, 1983.
Glengarry, Glen Ross. London: Methuen, 1984. New York: Grove Press, 1984.
Joseph Dintenfass. Unpublished, 1984.
The Shawl. Unpublished, 1985.

Filmscripts

The Postman Always Rings Twice. Unpublished, 1979.
The Verdict. Unpublished, 1981.

Things Change (in collaboration with Shel Silverstein). Unpublished, 1984.

SELECTED CRITICISM OF DAVID MAMET

Books

Bigsby, C. W. E. *A Critical Introduction to 20th Century American Drama*. Volume 3: *Beyond Broadway*. Cambridge: Cambridge University Press, 1985.

Cohn, Ruby. *New American Drama 1960–1980*. London: Macmillan, 1982.

Articles

Barbera, Jack V. 'Ethical Perversity in America: Some Observations on David Mamet's *American Buffalo*'. *Modern Drama*, 3 (September 1981), pp. 270–8.

Candullo, Bert. 'Comedy and *Sexual Perversity in Chicago*,' *Notes on Contemporary Literature*, 12, 1 (1982), p. 6.

Ditsky, John. 'He Lets You See the Thought There: The Theatre of David Mamet'. *Kansas Quarterly*, 12, 4 (1979), pp. 25–34.

Gale, Steven H. 'David Mamet's *The Duck Variations*', *Cue*, 59, 1 (Fall–Winter 1980), pp. 17–18.

Lewis, Patricia, and Browne, Terry. 'David Mamet'. *Dictionary of Literary Biography*, vol. 7 (1981), pp. 63–70.

Schleuter, June, and Forsyth, Elizabeth. 'America as Junkshop: The Business Ethic in David Mamet's *American Buffalo*'. *Modern Drama* (December 1983), pp. 492–500.

Storey, Robert. 'The Making of David Mamet'. *The Hollins Critic*, 16, 4 (1978), pp. 1–11.

Ventimiglia, Peter James. 'Recent Trends in American Drama: Michael Cristofer, David Mamet, and Albert Innaurato'. *Journal of American Culture* (Spring 1978), pp. 195–204.

For Product Safety Concerns and Information please contact our EU
representative GPSR@taylorandfrancis.com
Taylor & Francis Verlag GmbH, Kaufingerstraße 24, 80331 München, Germany

www.ingramcontent.com/pod-product-compliance
Lightning Source LLC
Chambersburg PA
CBHW052130300426
44116CB00010B/1844